WHAT IS TRUTH?

WHAT IS TRUTH?

Navigating a World of Faith, Science, and Noise

Aaron D. Franklin

DESERET
BOOK

SALT LAKE CITY, UTAH

Library of Congress Cataloging-in-Publication Data

Names: Franklin, Aaron (Professor of Electrical Engineering), author.
Title: What is truth? : navigating a world of faith, science, and noise / Aaron D. Franklin.
Description: Salt Lake City, Utah : Deseret Book, [2025] | Includes bibliographical references. | Summary: "Latter-day Saint and scientist Aaron D. Franklin explains how science and faith can be complementary of each other and not adversarial"—Provided by publisher.
Identifiers: LCCN 2024059442 (print) | LCCN 2024059443 (ebook) | ISBN 9781639934201 (hardback) | ISBN 9781649334381 (ebook)
Subjects: LCSH: Religion and science. | Truth—Religious aspects—The Church of Jesus Christ of Latter-day Saints.
Classification: LCC BL240.3 .F734 2025 (print) | LCC BL240.3 (ebook) | DDC 261.5/50882893—dc23/eng/20250203
LC record available at https://lccn.loc.gov/2024059442
LC ebook record available at https://lccn.loc.gov/2024059443

Printed in the United Sates of America
Publishers Printing, Salt Lake City, UT

10   9   8   7   6   5   4   3   2   1

To Ellie, Grant, and Blake.
I hope you always find strength, peace, and purpose
in choosing to believe.

CONTENTS

AUTHOR'S NOTE

We live in a time of mass information and rampant confusion. Regardless of the theology you embrace, the vocation you pursue, or the politics you espouse, to live in the world today is to feel the swarm of conflicting information touted as truth. I wrote this book to describe my view of the landscape of truth and falsehood, including examples from my life, and to offer what I have learned as a result. As a member of The Church of Jesus Christ of Latter-day Saints, my thoughts on finding truth draw heavily from this theological backdrop. A key doctrine of the Church is that God has made truth available from a variety of sources that include different religions, science, personal experience, and more. I wholeheartedly believe this.

To those who do not share my religious beliefs and are venturing into this book, I trust you will find more similarities than you may at first anticipate. You will also get some insight into how I, as a deeply religious member of The Church of Jesus Christ of Latter-day Saints and as a dedicated scientist and professor, personally navigate faith and science amid the noise and pressures of the world. I have experienced the thrill of discovering truth and the confusion of finding contradictions in all aspects of my life. My hope is that something learned through my struggles may provide help for another who is wrestling with their own uncertainty or doubt.

It is perfectly acceptable—and even likely—that you may have different views than those I share on any topic discussed herein. None of our differences needs to compromise this one principle: we are all doing our best to navigate a world of distractions and confusion in search of truth. The journey is best when we respect each other as fellow travelers, appreciating differences without depreciating the value of those who hold them.

PREFACE

A fun party game I've played at many group gatherings is "Two Truths and a Lie." In this game, a person shares three "facts" about themselves with the group—two of which are true and one that is a lie, hence the name. The goal of the person in the hot seat is to choose these "facts" in such a way that it's difficult for the group to identify the lie. Then the group's objective is to accurately determine which statement is false by asking questions and debating. In addition to some shock and laughter, the game usually ends with the person sharing the stories behind the two things that are actually true.

With the ground rules in place, let's play a round. Here are my two truths and a lie (in no particular order, of course):

(1) I flunked out of college.
(2) I'm an experienced skydiver.
(3) I proposed to my wife over the phone.

Since you probably don't know much about me, and you can't ask me questions about these, I have a serious advantage here. I've selected things that are relatively rare, and each may seem surprising. Have you made your selection? Which of the three do you think is the lie? The answer is "(2) I'm an experienced skydiver." I chose this lie carefully because I have been skydiving—once—but I'm not actually experienced. As for the other two statements, which are true, there's a story behind each that provides important context to the isolated fact. I feel particularly vulnerable revealing the one about proposing to my wife over the phone—I promise I can explain! My explanation may not be entirely satisfactory, and my wife might still have feelings about this poor choice more than twenty years later; but, hey—she did say yes!

The fact that I really did flunk out of college is often the most surprising for people who know that my current occupation is as a professor at a major university. These two facts seem so incongruent that one might wonder how they could both be true. Or if someone believes I'm unqualified as a professor (let's not poll my students right after they take a midterm!), their instinct might be to embrace the idea that I was a college dropout because it supports their internal narrative about me. This is just a small example of the battles we face each moment when presented with new information: Do we care about the information? Do we have any personal experience with it? Does it align with our assumptions and existing beliefs?

Often what keeps us from recognizing the truth is a mismatch between new information and our expectations. For those who know me only as a professor, it's hard to believe I flunked out of college. But for those who knew me only when I flunked out, it's hard to believe I'm now a professor! Our experiences shape certain expectations, and we must carefully navigate these in our search for what's true.

The point of all this is that finding truth can be challenging, whether it's about a person, about the world around us, or about God. What makes matters worse is that we live in an era filled with masterfully disguised lies. These lies are rarely outright falsehoods with no connection to the truth—that would make them too obvious. For instance, if my one lie had been, "I am the prime minister of the United Kingdom," you could easily determine that it's not true based on what you know (e.g., who the current prime minister actually is). Conversely, most of the falsehoods we encounter every day are camouflaged with just enough facts to slip through most filters.

In my own search for truth, I have experienced a wide range of contrasts: from being a college dropout to a college graduate; from being a completely irreligious person to a fully committed believer; and from being a pupil of scientific learning to a scientist making new discoveries. Throughout this journey, I've discovered certain core truths related to God, His plan for us as His children, and the ways He works among us; these truths are of greatest importance to me. I've also found that in order to identify greater truth in other aspects of my life, I am most balanced and happy when I protect my core truths, learn about others' beliefs with openness, and never place what someone *believes* above who they *are* as a child of God.

While I'm a convert to The Church of Jesus Christ of Latter-day Saints—I joined as a young teenager—my deep appreciation for the truth I found in the restored gospel came when I served as a full-time missionary in Atlanta, Georgia. Before my mission, I knew I had received confirmations from the Spirit of the truthfulness of the Book of Mormon, but I had not fully appreciated how clear and compelling our message was until I began sharing it with others. Instead of trying to persuade people with historical facts, social pressure, or other convincing features, we extended the invitation of a lifetime to everyone we met: "Would you like to *know the truth for yourself?*" We provided them with the tools, instructed them on the process, and testified from our own experience that if they would move forward with faith and seek confirmation, they would receive their own personal witness of the truth "by the power of the Holy Ghost" (Moroni 10:5).

It wasn't just the uniqueness of our invitation that compelled me as a missionary. It was also the message from the prophet of the Church at the time, President Gordon B. Hinckley. While I was serving my mission, he addressed the National Press Club in Washington, DC, and spoke about the Church's approach to interfaith relations: "You bring all the good that you have and let us see if we can add to it."*

This recognition that there is truth to be found in the theology, experiences, education, and perspectives of those outside my religion felt so appropriate and correct for understanding this vast and varied planet. It just made so much sense of the world. I knew there was such goodness in so many people who believed differently than I did, and President Hinckley's counsel made it clear that they also have truth. Even within God's restored Church on earth, there remains an ongoing need for "many great and important things pertaining to the Kingdom of God" (Articles of Faith 1:9) to be revealed. While one obvious way these great and important things are revealed is through latter-day prophets, who's to say that some of them won't come from joining hands with those of other theologies from across the globe?

That brings me to why I wrote this book. I believe that The Church of Jesus Christ of Latter-day Saints contains the fulness of the gospel of Jesus Christ, and that the attributes of God, the Father of all, are captured in the scriptures and core doctrines of the Church. I have been through trials of faith where my confidence in this knowledge was deeply tested amid torrents of information or hardship, but my conviction has weathered the storms and emerged stronger. I have also come to know that there are magnificent truths revealed through science, from modern digital technology to our growing understanding of the cosmos. There are glorious truths brought to light through many other fields of study, the arts, and the lived experiences of billions of

---

* Gordon B. Hinckley, address to the National Press Club, Washington, DC, March 8, 2000; in *Discourses of President Gordon B. Hinckley* (Salt Lake City: Deseret Book, 2005), 2:581. This sentiment was repeated in President Hinckley's October 2002 general conference talk, "The Marvelous Foundation of Our Faith": "Bring with you all that you have of good and truth which you have received from whatever source, and come and let us see if we may add to it" (*Ensign*, November 2002).

people. Additionally, there are inspiring truths held by faithful members of countless other religions across the globe.

Sadly, all this incredible truth is clouded by an onslaught of dishonesty, deception, and distraction. I have sat with many members of the Church of Jesus Christ and listened as they described doubting things they once believed they knew. Meanwhile, people from all walks of life are confused about what is real and what is fake in the relentless flood of information and misinformation. This book is not a definitive, stand-alone solution for navigating this storm. If there were an easy, straightforward answer in the form of a universal truth detector, we wouldn't be in such confusion today. I believe part of the divinely intended growth we experience in this mortal life comes by navigating these complexities.

This book is meant to offer a perspective on truth—where it comes from and what it represents. By appreciating the various sources of truth, including those we may not often consider, our capacity for understanding greater truths will increase. My hope is that this book will motivate seekers of truth to achieve a balance of openness without compromising their confidence in core truths they have come to know. While I strive to not get overly philosophical, we do explore the nature of truth and how to know if you truly *know* something, particularly when it comes to the truths in the gospel of Jesus Christ. I hope you find reassurance and hope in the principles, stories, and recommendations within these pages, and can more confidently approach the frequently asked question: "What is truth?"

Chapter 1

INTRODUCTION TO TRUTH

Where is the wisdom we have lost in knowledge?
Where is the knowledge we have lost in information?
—T. S. Eliot

Space fascinates me. I'm all the flavors of space nerd: NASA, *Star Trek*, *Star Wars* (in unranked order, of course). A few years ago, I decided it was time to take my interest in the cosmos to the next level and get a telescope. When you consider I'm a scientist, you may be surprised that I knew next to nothing about telescopes. There's a common assumption that a scientist should know, well, all science-y stuff. In reality, I've managed to horrify many a friend with my poor trivia knowledge of most scientific fields outside my own.

My wife came to the rescue. She responded to my interest in getting a telescope with one of the best gifts I've ever been given. It's not just that she bought me a telescope but that she invested hours and hours of her time reading about the differences between various models, comparing features, and digging through endless user reviews. Isn't this the misery of deciding to buy just about anything these days? Despite being decidedly not an astrophysicist, my wife's investment of time and study made her a far more knowledgeable and reliable source on telescope technology than her scientist husband.

When I unwrapped the large present to discover what I now understand is a Dobsonian reflector telescope with a six-inch aperture, I was so excited! Rather than being motorized and computer controlled, the telescope was intentionally manual to allow for the thrill (born of frustration) of finding celestial objects on your own. My wife had done an incredible job. In the months that followed, as I learned more about the telescope field, it became increasingly obvious she had made the perfect choice.

An unforgettable experience happened a few weeks after getting the telescope. It was a clear night with good "seeing,"* and I managed my first view of the planet Saturn. I was floored. Something about my own eye squinting into the eyepiece of the telescope I had personally set up and aimed at the sky seeing that small glowing object with a distinct ring around it changed me. All that I had learned about Saturn since I was a child—the pictures I'd seen, taken by far more powerful telescopes—faded as the reality of its existence reached me at an entirely new depth that night. And don't worry, being the obnoxious dad that I am, I dragged my grumbly teenage children out into the cold so they could also see for themselves. Despite the eyerolls and protests, I like to tell myself it was a wonderful memory for them.

This experience taught me something about truth that I hadn't previously considered: many things we accept as real have little to no basis in direct observation or personal experience. If you'd asked me prior to that chilly night whether Saturn was real, I would have answered with a confident, "Yes, of course," even though I'd never actually seen the planet for myself. Once I actually *saw* the distinctive ringed orb with my own eyes, my previous confidence felt lacking in comparison to my now far more solid certainty of Saturn's existence. What I'd previously

---

* This is astronomy lingo for conditions in the atmosphere being favorable for viewing distant astronomical objects through a telescope. Factors that influence "seeing" include light pollution, humidity, atmospheric turbulence, local conditions, telescope optics, and many others. Next time you find yourself in an astronomy club, you'll know what they mean when they say the seeing was good over the weekend!

thought I *knew*, I'd actually *believed*—a distinction I was unaware of until I saw Saturn for myself.

What Is Real?

Let's pull this thread of questioning the certainty of what is real or true a bit further. If you were asked to rate, on a scale of 1 to 10, how real Antarctica is, with 10 being certain it's real and 1 being certain it's not real, what would your rating be? Take a moment and give some thought to your answer before continuing to read.

I'm guessing your rating was somewhere between 7 and 10. After all, the question probably struck you initially as quite strange. Maybe you reacted with the thought: "Of course it's real—what a silly question!" You've seen maps showing Antarctica, heard stories of explorers venturing there, and been taught it's one of seven continents on Earth. But if its existence is so certain, then why would I have asked that question? Based on the experience I just shared about Saturn, you may be rethinking how confident you are in the realness of Antarctica. That realization might have led you to reduce your initial 10 down to a solid—but open-minded—8.

Have you actually been to Antarctica? Ever set foot on its mostly glacial surface? Have you even seen it for yourself, perhaps from a trip to the International Space Station? Across the entirety of human history, only a staggeringly low 0.0005 percent of people have actually seen or visited Antarctica.† That's only one in every 200,000 people who have ever lived on Earth! How would your "realness" score change if you were one of the 0.0005 percent?

---

† Estimate based on an approximation of 100,000 tourists visiting Antarctica each year in recent years (mostly via expedition cruising), for a total of about 500,000. Another 10,000 scientists and workers have been on the continent over time and a little fewer than 700 people have been to space, with only a subset of those being in a position to see Antarctica. Total human population is estimated to be about 108 billion across all history, yielding the ~0.0005 percent.

When I posed this thought experiment to a youth Sunday School class, one young woman gave a confident answer of 10. I asked her why she was so sure, and she said, "Because my uncle has been there and told us all about it." I then asked the rest of the class whether any of them would like to change their realness rating now that they knew someone whose uncle has been to Antarctica. Some did. Some did not.

Planets and Continents—What About Daily Confusion?

The point of our examination of the reality or truth of something is that, when pressed, our previously confident foundations can become shaky. Prior to reading the previous section, you likely never questioned the reality of Antarctica, but now maybe you do, even just a little. While I didn't provide a counterpoint suggesting Antarctica doesn't actually exist, I may have at least caused you to question whether you're totally confident in the supporting evidence you've received. Perhaps I forced you to consider the realness of things on a scale rather than as a simple binary of *yes* or *no*.

But let's face it, most of us don't spend our time pondering the reality of planets or continents. What's most perplexing is the uncertainty of everything around us every day. Between generative artificial intelligence (AI), endless reels across any number of social media platforms, and loud declarations of political or social points of view, it's no wonder that truth feels slippery to many. Those who push back and declare with confidence that *their* understanding of a topic or situation is definitively true can lead others to wonder if they're considering the full picture from all perspectives. In some cases, those with the most confidence spend little time outside of the metaphorical echo chambers of one-sided, reciprocal thought.

Besides the expansiveness of all that's transpired across history, which we continue to seek to understand, there's a staggering amount of information generated on a daily basis. YouTube alone sees millions of hours of video uploaded daily, not to mention the nearly one trillion emails sent and received each day. Recent trends suggest we are generating approximately 22 percent more data each year than the previous year.* What's the big deal? Why does the volume of data being generated matter? Surely you don't care about the vast majority of this data, right? Perhaps, but none of us can escape the ramifications of this data existing. A certain amount of the information will contain falsehoods, and these will be embraced and amplified by some as truth. For others, an earnest search for truth will result in a combination of some facts and some lies, assembled into an attractive and compelling narrative. Just as you're beginning to sort out how something fits together, another 400 million terabytes of data are created the next day—and the next, and the next.

This onslaught brings to mind the power and simplicity found in Joshua's words related to holding fast to an unshakable core: "*Choose you this day whom ye will serve*; whether the gods which your fathers served that were on the other side of the flood, or the gods of the Amorites, in whose land ye dwell: but as for me and my house, *we will serve the Lord*" (Joshua 24:15; emphasis added). No matter how much data, or how many options there are, or how loud the voices, or how massive the number of followers, it ultimately comes down to a personal choice.

No matter the topic, what we choose to believe is true depends largely on the integrity of the sources and personal experiences we've had with it. Family members, religious leaders, and political figures are often relied upon as the fountains of the truth we choose to uphold, with little thought about whether their declarations come from a place of actual truth. I'm not suggesting that relying on such luminaries is inherently or universally wrong—there's really no getting around some level of dependence on what we deem to be trusted sources. Rather, what

---

* Information throughout this paragraph comes from Fabio Duarte, "Amount of Data Created Daily (2024), *Exploding Topics* (website); https://explodingtopics.com/blog /data-generated-per-day#; accessed 16 October 2024.

I hope to relay throughout this book are three guiding principles that can make navigating the sea of uncertainty and doubt easier, particularly when we are pressed to question whether we've come to know something for ourselves and not only by believing others. These principles are intentionally paired with the three essential components for developing a faith that leads to salvation according to *Lectures on Faith*,[1] namely

(1) God is the ultimate source of all truth. *Lectures on Faith* calls this a correct idea of God's attributes.
(2) Knowing truth requires choosing to believe, no matter the topic. *Lectures on Faith* states this as "believe God exists."
(3) We cannot comprehend all the things God comprehends. *Lectures on Faith* sees this as knowledge that our course in life is aligned with God's will.

We'll go through each of these points individually.

Principle 1
God Is the Ultimate Source of All Truth

Lectures on Faith 3:4—"A *correct* idea of [God's] attributes"

Amid the flood of information, divergent interpretations, and constant noise, we have an ultimate source of *all* truth: our omniscient God. It was the Savior who taught that knowing "the truth shall make you free" (John 8:32).[*] Free from what? Well, most importantly, free from the bondage of sin. In a most complete way, this verse is alluding to capital *T* Truth,[†] meaning the Son of God, our Savior and Redeemer.

---

[*] It's telling that Jesus spoke these words to "those Jews which believed on him" (John 8:31). Choosing to believe unlocks a level of access when it comes to truth, and when it is God we are choosing to believe in, that access includes, eventually, the truth of all things.

[†] In their book, *Who Is Truth?* (Verdand Press, 2019), Jeffrey L. Thayne and Edwin E. Gantt provide a wonderfully thorough description of the differences between Greek and Hebrew thoughts on truth, where one side (Greek) sees truth as related to fixed

It is knowing Him, including His character and attributes, that will ultimately free us from sin and bondage (see John 14:6). By coming to know Him, we become more like Him, "abundant in goodness and truth" (Exodus 34:6).

Importantly, it's not just that God is the source of all truth that should satisfy us, but more so that He has promised access to His infinite source via the Holy Ghost, also known as the "Spirit of truth" (John 16:13). One of the most oft-quoted scriptures regarding finding truth is found in Moroni 10:5: "And by the power of the Holy Ghost ye may know the truth of all things."

We can take this one step further based on teachings from Peter in the New Testament:

> Knowing this first, that no prophecy of the scripture is of any private interpretation.
>
> For the prophecy came not in old time by the will of man: but holy men of God spake as they were moved by the Holy Ghost. (2 Peter 1:20–21)

The prophecies and teachings of scripture and modern prophets provide another conduit for accessing the all-encompassing source of truth, which stems from God. This can be broadly termed the "word of God." As Elder David A. Bednar taught:

> Let me suggest that holding fast to the word of God entails (1) remembering, honoring, and strengthening the personal connection we have with the Savior and His Father through the covenants and ordinances of the restored gospel and (2) prayerfully, earnestly,

---

ideas and specifics about what transpires while the other side (Hebrew) sees truth as a person with context and the ability to change. By way of Hebrew thought, Jesus is the capital *T* Truth that we must come to know. There is so much more to this compelling perspective on Truth that is explored beautifully in Thayne and Gantt's book.

and consistently using the holy scriptures and the teachings of living prophets and apostles as sure sources of revealed truth.[2]

With the restored gospel of Jesus Christ, we not only acknowledge that God is the ultimate source of truth, but we also have tangible access to His word and the encouragement to hold fast to it as we press forward through the storms of life.

Principle 2
Knowing Truth Requires Choosing to Believe, No Matter the Topic

Lectures on Faith 3:3—Believe "that [God] actually exists"

Unless we are the actual source of truth for a particular thing, we will ultimately have to choose whether to believe. For instance, Joseph Smith was the source of truth regarding the First Vision—he is the one who went into the woods and experienced what he experienced. For the rest of us, there is his word, the word of others who support his telling of events, and the word of some who ardently decry his claims. Your personal conviction for one view of the First Vision or another is going to ultimately be driven by where you choose to place your belief. While there may be personal witnesses sought and obtained from the Holy Spirit, combined with a collection of trustworthy sources offering their position, your own personal rating of the realness of the First Vision will still depend on where you choose to place your belief—including in your own personal witnesses!

Believing in something can bring tremendous power. I've only recently come to appreciate this reality. There are many settings where the declaration of "knowing" something to be true is overused; there seems to be a sense that professing only belief in something is somehow weaker. I would contend that believing in something is one of the most powerful, personal acts of faith we can offer. There are numerous examples of this throughout the scriptures; allow me to offer just one.

When Nephi *believed* the Lord was able to make the things his father saw known unto him, he found himself "caught away in the Spirit of the Lord" (1 Nephi 11:1). The Spirit appeared to Nephi and had a full conversation with him; think of this for a moment, an actual verbal back-and-forth conversation directly with the Spirit!

> And the Spirit said unto me: Believest thou that thy father saw the tree of which he hath spoken?
>
> And I said: Yea, thou knowest that I believe all the words of my father. (1 Nephi 11:4–5)

The Spirit, who knows "the truth of all things" (Moroni 10:5), asked Nephi whether he believed that his father saw the tree of life. Isn't that fascinating? I attribute this to the power that accompanies professions of belief. Nephi's declaration that he believes everything his father taught (and, further, that the Spirit knows this) clearly unlocked a level of power and accompanied joy that is rarely matched in all of scripture. Not only did this profession of belief ultimately unlock a vision that included seeing the Savior, but also led to a powerful expression of joy by the Spirit in the next verse:

> And when I had spoken these words, the Spirit cried with a loud voice, saying: Hosanna to the Lord, the most high God; for he is God over all the earth, yea, even above all. And blessed art thou, Nephi, *because thou believest* in the Son of the most high God; wherefore, thou shalt behold the things which thou hast desired. (1 Nephi 11:6; emphasis added)

Isn't the Spirit typically the soft and subtle voice? Not this time! Nephi's profession of belief led to a loud hosanna to God! I trust that there is similar celebration in the heavens when we choose to believe.

Influences around us may pressure in one direction or another, but ours is the only hand on the lever of belief within our soul; ultimately, we are the only ones who know what we truly believe.

Principle 3
We Cannot Comprehend All the
Lord Can Comprehend

Lectures on Faith 3:5—A knowledge that our "course of life" is aligned with God

One of the most oft-cited conversion stories in all of scriptures is that of the people of King Benjamin in Mosiah 2–5. There are many inspiring aspects to their conversion, including that they "had viewed themselves in their own carnal state, even less than the dust of the earth" (Mosiah 4:2). In utter humility, they cried out together for mercy, declaring, "we *believe* in Jesus Christ, the Son of God, who created heaven and earth, and all things" (Mosiah 4:2; emphasis added). This verbal profession of belief is what appears to have been the triggering point, and "after they had spoken these words the Spirit of the Lord came upon them, and they were filled with joy, having received a remission of their sins, and having peace of conscience" (Mosiah 4:3).*

A few verses later, King Benjamin notes that they have come to a *knowledge* of God's goodness and matchless power (see Mosiah 4:6). Yet this knowledge will not be enough. There is something fundamental that must be a new constant for them, something that cannot simply be a one-time occurrence. He spells it out here:

> *Believe* in God; *believe* that he is, and that he created all things, both in heaven and in earth; *believe* that he has all wisdom, and all

---

* Here is yet another instance where a profession of belief triggers an outpouring of spiritual manifestations. There is great power in choosing to believe, then expressing that belief (i.e., acting in faith).

power, both in heaven and in earth; *believe* that man doth not comprehend all the things which the Lord can comprehend. (Mosiah 4:9; emphasis added)

No matter how much we learn, how much we experience, or even how much we come to know, there will still be a need for our belief. There is clear and present danger in imagining that we're able to comprehend all the things God can comprehend, which would eliminate our dependence on Him. As Jacob teaches, "it is impossible that man should find out all his ways" (Jacob 4:8). Yet, the more we learn, the more we're capable of, and the less we feel dependent on God and His infinite knowledge and power. I'm convinced that anyone who digs deeply enough will ultimately realize how limited their grasp of the whole truth really is. There is a famous quote attributed to a renowned scientist that says, "The first gulp from the glass of natural sciences will turn you into an atheist, but at the bottom of the glass God is waiting for you."†

Through the restored gospel of Jesus Christ, we know the God that fills the gaps where science cannot answer, but He is far more than just a mystical placeholder—He is a personal, long-suffering, all-powerful Father who seeks for all to come to know Him, and thus to know all truth. King Benjamin taught his people to actively believe in an all-powerful God, and that they should seek to help and bless and serve

---

† Attribution of this quote is tricky. Typically, it's attributed to Werner Heisenberg, a famous German physicist and one of the pioneers of quantum mechanics. However, it does not appear in any of his published writings. Some have surmised that the quote echoes sentiments from Francis Bacon and Alexander Pope more closely than Heisenberg. Truth is (pun intended), it's unclear who said it, but it's still spot on for making this point! I once shared this quote during a class I was teaching, and one of the attendees shared the following with me afterward: "I think the first gulp of *anything* that is very painful or the first gulp of experiences that challenge our expectations in a very aggressive way can also have you wondering if God is there . . . but at the bottom of the glass, and I mean the very bottom at times, He is waiting."

others "for the sake of retaining a remission of [their] sins from day to day, that [they] may walk guiltless before God" (Mosiah 4:26).

As we choose to believe in God, make and keep covenants with Him, and strive to learn His attributes and character—while recognizing that we cannot comprehend all that God comprehends—our confidence that we are on the path He would have us walk will grow. This formula embodies the three requirements for "exercising faith in God unto life and salvation."[3]

Applying the Principles

Throughout this book, the end of each chapter will include a section titled "Applying the Principles" to provide a concise list of some practical applications and key takeaways from what was discussed. My hope is that these actionable steps will reinforce the core messages of the chapter, helping you integrate the concepts presented into your daily life, guiding your actions, decisions, and spiritual growth as you seek to find, understand, and live by truth.

1. **Seek personal experience:** Whenever possible, seek to validate truths through your own experiences or learning. Like viewing Saturn through a telescope, personal encounters with truth solidify and deepen your understanding. For gospel truths, this requires living the truth with faith, which will open the way for confirmation from the Spirit.

2. **Acknowledge the role of believing:** Recognize that not all truth can be empirically proven. Faith plays a critical role in accepting certain truths, particularly in spiritual matters. This may include trusting in reliable sources or witnesses, particularly at first. When it comes to core truths of the gospel of Jesus Christ, recognize that belief brings blessings.

3. **Build confidence and value in God's truth:** Strengthen your

confidence in truths that come from God, knowing that they are more certain and enduring than any worldly knowledge. What small changes could you make in your daily life to demonstrate how you prioritize gospel truths?

4. **Embrace humility in learning:** Approach all learning with humility, recognizing there is always more to discover and understand, especially from God's infinite wisdom. Never let what you know diminish your reliance on God and your comparative nothingness without Him.

It's no secret that we live in a time when truth is slippery and falsehoods abound. Many profess to know things they do not know, while others are assumed to know things they have not learned. Despite all the noise and deluge of information, *there is truth and much of it is accessible.* The overarching principles of God's omniscience, the power of choosing to believe, and the realization that we cannot comprehend all that God comprehends should guide us on our path to truth. But what is the path? How do we navigate it? Is there a way to filter through the incessant noise of information? What impact do the different sources of truth, including science and religion, have on what we believe? These are the types of questions we will explore throughout this book, with the hope of gaining a greater understanding of the sources of truth and how to find and embrace the truth of all things with lasting confidence.

Chapter 2

THE PARABLE OF THE FISH SCIENTISTS

We're just working with the tools God gave us. There's no reason that science and religion have to operate in an adversarial relationship. Both come from the same source, the only source of truth—the Creator.

—Joseph E. Murray

Conferences are a standard feature of the scientific world. It doesn't matter whether the field of study is entomology, anthropology, cosmology, or nanotechnology—there are scientific conferences to choose from, and not just for the disciplines that end in *-ology*.* Besides the commonality of such meetings existing across different fields, certain features are almost always present: technical sessions where researchers present their results, active discussions in the hallways and at social gatherings, and copious amounts of alcohol at receptions.

I attend about ten conferences in my field every year. Based on some quick math and a few assumptions, I estimate that I've sat through over 10,000 presentations of research results! One of the most memorable

---

* While difficult to know exactly how many scientific conferences are held each year, with an estimate of 8.4 million researchers worldwide (see S. Sarabipour et al., *Nature Human Behaviour*, vol. 5 [2021]: 296), each attending three to four conferences per year in their respective fields with an average attendance of 300 (some much larger and some much smaller), a rough guess would be approximately 100,000 scientific conferences being held around the world each year.

things that happened while I attended one of these thousands of presentations occurred several years ago. During the large plenary session, an elderly gentleman in the audience began snoring loudly. At first, there were chuckles of laughter from those sitting nearby, but the giggles turned to gasps when the man suddenly stopped breathing! The student sitting next to him began attempting CPR while the man was still seated in the middle of the crowded lecture hall with steeply graded rows. When the seated CPR proved unsuccessful, several attendees managed to hoist the man up and proceed to pass him, crowd-surfing style, to the front of the hall. As they were lowering him to the ground, he suddenly started breathing again and sat up, looking very confused. Paramedics arrived and whisked him off to the hospital. As he was being wheeled out on a stretcher, the elderly scientist gave a thumbs-up to the audience, and everyone applauded, relieved to see him breathing and coherent. The room fell silent for a few minutes after the paramedics departed, and then the presenter awkwardly resumed his scientific presentation from where he had left off. The person sitting next to me leaned over and whispered, "Well, until today I'd never actually seen someone literally bored to death."†

As for the open bars during receptions at scientific conferences, I've found they provide more opportunities to discuss my faith than almost any other setting. To socialize in these settings with a fizzy glass of Coca-Cola in your hand is like wearing a neon sign that says, "Ask me why I'm different!" As a naturally high-energy person, I once had a very engaging and animated group discussion at a conference reception. Afterward, a fellow professor told me I was "the most fun sober person" he'd ever met. I've since thought about memorializing that on a T-shirt.

During one conference reception, I was asked the expected question

---

† Don't get me wrong, there have also been exhilarating presentations at scientific conferences! But it may be a stretch to suggest they're the norm.

about why I don't drink alcohol, and I provided the well-worn answer: "For religious reasons—I'm a member of The Church of Jesus Christ of Latter-day Saints." This seemed to stun the person for a moment. They remarked they had known several members of my church over the years and were curious about how I'm able to balance the scientific reality of things with my religious beliefs. This wasn't the typical follow-up question I'd come to expect. In all the conference receptions and dinner events I'd been to over the years, the responses were either changing the topic or a few basic questions about the Church, whether I had served a mission, that sort of thing.

Despite the uniqueness of the question, my response came quickly. "It's simple," I said. "I don't compartmentalize. Truth is truth. Some of it I discover following scientific methods in the lab with empirical evidence, while other truths I discover by exercising faith in my life with experiential evidence."

Since that interaction, I've given more thought to the question I was asked amid a crowd of inebriated scientists. While my abstention from the free alcohol might have been the most obvious difference, there was something much deeper which set me apart from many of my peers— my view of truth. Over the years, I've learned that while many scientists do believe in God, blending the scientific and religious worlds can be seen as taboo to some. To me, however, they're inseparable.

Consider the following parable that illustrates this principle more fully. Since you now know more than you ever wanted to know about scientific conferences and a few of my experiences attending them, it should come as no surprise that the parable involves scientists and a conference. While it is admittedly silly compared to the deeply relevant and inspiring parables* the Savior used to teach truth, I hope it will provide some meaningful value and messaging regarding truth.

---

* To be entirely accurate in terminology here, what I present is perhaps more a moral story than a parable. I'd like to think there is deep meaning and applicability in the story

The Parable of the Fish Scientists

In a world where little was known about fish, a scientist moved into a cabin by a river. The landscape was beautiful—the river winding through a dense forest of trees that offered seclusion. The isolation was what this scientist craved, as there was much work to do. The winding river just outside his door was teeming with fish, which he had come to study.

The fish scientist went right to work. He began fishing the river and catching dazzlingly striped fish. Through meticulous experimentation, he discovered which bait the fish preferred at certain times of day or types of weather (see Figure 1A). Carefully, he dissected the fish and studied their anatomy. He even baked, fried, boiled, and smoked the fish to understand how they tasted. As a scientist, he was methodical and thorough, investing years of his life in the careful study and documentation of the striped fish.

Finally, the time came for the fish scientist to do what any self-respecting scientist would do: present his findings at a scientific

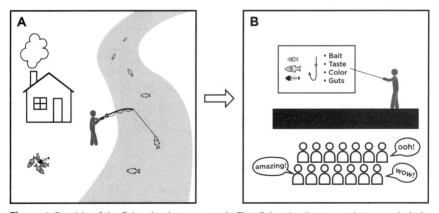

Figure 1. Parable of the fish scientists—part 1. **A:** First fish scientist moves into a secluded cabin by a river and catches the striped fish, dissecting and eating them. **B:** He presents his findings at a fish conference.

(hence, *parable*), but more than anything, it presents a fairly straightforward moral (hence *moral story*) regarding differing methods of discovering truth.

conference! After carefully preparing the presentation detailing his many discoveries, he traveled to the big city for the conference. When his time to speak arrived, he nervously took the stage to present to the world the findings he had dedicated years of his life to uncover. He presented the details of how to catch the fish, the meticulous aspects of their anatomy, and even his observations of how they taste prepared in various ways. As the drawing in Figure 1B shows, the audience was amazed, stunned, wowed, gobsmacked—hey, isn't that what always happens at scientific conferences? They knew they'd learned things that were never known before.

At the conclusion of his talk, the fish scientist returned to his seat amid exuberant (albeit professional) applause. While he was still glowing with joy about how well his findings had been received, the next speaker took the stage. It was another fish scientist. The audience calmed and listened as the second fish scientist described how *she* had moved into a cabin by a large lake. She spent years studying the striped fish that lived in this lake, following entirely different methodologies from the first fish scientist. Rather than catching the fish with bait and studying their anatomy, the second fish scientist would scuba dive in the lake and observe the fish in their natural habitat (see Figure 2A). She documented their behavior and life cycle, including how some would leave the lake area and not return. After catching some fish with a net, she kept them in a tank in her cabin to further examine their traits, all the while conducting thorough studies.

As this second fish scientist explained her many findings, the audience was once again astonished and thrilled! That is, all but one. As seen in Figure 2B, the first fish scientist was flabbergasted! "What nonsense is this?" he exclaimed at the conclusion of the talk. During the break, the two fish scientists met in the hallway and engaged in an animated debate over the question, "What is the striped fish?" (see Figure 3). The fish scientist who performed his studies by the river was adamant that the

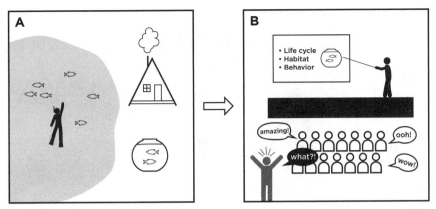

Figure 2. Parable of the fish scientists—part 2. **A:** Second fish scientist moves into a cabin by a lake and observes the striped fish in their habitat, including their life cycle and behavior. **B:** She presents her findings at the fish conference, amazing all in the audience except for the first fish scientist.

truth about the striped fish was found in the fish's preference for certain bait, their anatomy, and how they tasted when cooked. Meanwhile, the fish scientist who carefully studied by the lake insisted that the truth about the striped fish was found in their life cycle, behavior, and habitat.

"You can't possibly study a fish without catching and dissecting it!" the first insisted.

"You learn nothing about a fish once you've killed it!" the second retorted.

Both scientists were convinced the other was either lying (deceived) or not actually talking about the same fish at all. One thing was clear to each: the methodology the other used did not produce truth.

The conference ended with no resolution reached between the two fish scientists. While the rest of the audience left feeling inspired and having their knowledge expanded by the truth provided by both scientists, the scientists themselves returned to their respective homes *knowing nothing more than they had when they left to attend the meeting.* They never realized that the river flowed into the lake. All along, they'd

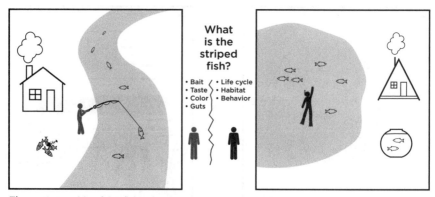

Figure 3. Parable of the fish scientists—part 3. The two fish scientists debate the question, "What is the fish?" Both are determined that their findings provide the only explanation about striped fish and the other scientist is deceived and misleading the world.

been less than a mile apart, studying and discovering truth about the same exact fish, just using different methodologies (see Figure 4).

The Moral

Well, aside from the obvious fact that you should definitely make a point of attending a scientific conference or two—they're exciting!—the moral of this parable relates to the many different methodologies for discovering truth. Then-Elder Russell M. Nelson's counsel on this topic, provided at the dedication of the Brigham Young University Life Sciences Building, sums this up well:

> All truth is part of the gospel of Jesus Christ. Whether truth comes from a scientific laboratory or by revelation from the Lord, it is compatible. . . . There is no conflict between science and religion. Conflict only arises from an incomplete knowledge of either science or religion—or both.[1]

I'm sure it's obvious my parable of the fish scientists teaches the importance of both scientific and religious or gospel truth—they both contribute to one great whole of all truth. I hope you go even further

Figure 4. Parable of the fish scientists—part 4. The two fish scientists never realized they lived less than a mile apart and had been studying the exact same fish, just using different methodologies that reveal distinct truths, in the same manner that science and religion (and many other methodologies) function in our search for truth.

than this, though. More generally, the parable teaches we should not discount truth obtained using methodologies that differ from ones we happen to be experienced in. Nor should we be instantly dismissive of information that at first seems contradictory to beliefs we currently hold. Many findings seen initially as contrary or paradoxical ultimately are found to be complementary *when understood completely*. Or even if not found to be complementary, allowing ourselves space to consider such contraries can ultimately lead us to greater truth, as the Prophet Joseph Smith taught: "By proving contraries, truth is made manifest."*

---

* Joseph Smith, "Letter to Israel Daniel Rupp, 5 June 1844," 1; spelling modernized. The Joseph Smith Papers; available at https://www.josephsmithpapers.org/paper-summary /letter-to-israel-daniel-rupp-5-june-1844/1; accessed 24 October 2024. Dr. Jared Halverson has many excellent insights about proving contraries that he has shared in different forums. He emphasizes the importance of recognizing and wrestling with polarities to uncover deeper truths, and how understanding and balancing opposing forces or ideas can lead to personal growth and a more profound grasp of our own faith. For example, see his interview on the *Faith Matters* podcast episode titled "Proving Polarities—A Conversation with Jared Halverson"; available at https://faithmatters.org /proving-polarities-a-conversation-with-jared-halverson/.

The fish scientist who was catching and dissecting the fish felt challenged by what the other fish scientist suggested regarding the fish's behavior, as if information about the fish's life cycle somehow upended information about their anatomy. From the parable, the ridiculousness seems obvious. But what about the application—is it as obvious or simple? Take, for instance, your personally held belief or findings related to something. Have you ever felt challenged in those truths by what someone else presented as their truths? Are you open to learning from someone who has a different theology, political party, medical opinion, or favorite sports team than you? If you are not, it may be worth reexamining the premise upon which you're making that sweeping decision of dismissiveness.

Here's an example most people are familiar with: Someone with a long-held belief in creationism as taught and interpreted literally from the book of Genesis (e.g., creation occurred in six days and the Earth is about 6,000 years old) may feel challenged by the scientific picture of the big bang and the theory of evolution. The creationist likely does not remember being present for the creation—no firsthand witnessing of what transpired—but holds their belief as fundamental to their faith based on how it has been taught, and based on personal spiritual witnesses interpreted as supportive of this view. Meanwhile, the evolutionist supporting the theory of evolution similarly has no firsthand witnesses of the event but has collected their data from numerous scientific studies of the universe and determined that the evidence tells a story of billions of years of evolution after an unimaginably massive energy explosion.

What do these two positions have in common? They're both working to describe how the world and life came to be. Yet they have both gone about developing their truth using different methodologies, the creationist with religious scripture, teaching, and personal revelation; and the evolutionist with scientific data, mathematical analysis, and observation. So, who's right and who's wrong? Could they possibly *both* be right, like the two fish scientists, both studying the same fish but using entirely different methodologies, and thus both providing important insights to the whole truth?*

I'm not going to answer these questions. My intent is to have you thinking along these lines. The example of creationist versus evolutionist is one of the most well-known, but there are countless others, and I hope some from your personal life have come to mind. It's not always science versus religion, but can also be differing religious views and interpretations, differing lived experiences and worldviews, differing historical interpretations, and so forth. Let's explore ways to frame our view of truth to account for the competing perspectives and experiences that surround us.

To reemphasize, this parable is not exclusive to "science" and "religion" as if these are the only methodological sources for truth. There is truth—and methods for discovering it—in all aspects of life, from history to the arts, athletics to nature, personal experience to societal development, and everything in between. The point is none of these should be viewed as fiefdoms of superiority or exclusivity when it comes to truth, and for those that recognize the importance of all truth, there should be a general openness to finding and understanding as much of it as possible (see Doctrine and Covenants 88:118).

---

* For an excellent talk on this topic see: Jamie L. Jensen, "Faith and Science: Symbiotic Pathways to Truth," BYU devotional, 3 November 2020; available at speeches.byu.edu. One of the points Jensen raises is the need to be comfortable with some uncertainty: "Dogmatism in science or in religion closes down your ability to learn and progress. If something seems to conflict between what science reveals and what you have learned through your religious faith, don't abandon one or the other. Hold off judgment, be patient, and keep an open mind to truth from both sides." Jensen also has a recent book on the subject: Jamie L. Jensen and Seth M. Bybee, *Let's Talk About Science and Religion* (Salt Lake City: Deseret Book Company, 2023).

Applying the Principles

1. **Seek truth from multiple sources:** Recognize that different methodologies (scientific and religious are just two of the many that exist!) can reveal different aspects of truth. Be open to insights from both faith and empirical evidence.

2. **Avoid dismissing contrary views:** When confronted with perspectives that differ from your own, approach them with openness rather than immediate dismissal. Avoid dogmatism. Consider how another perspective might complement rather than contradict your understanding. Be patient with some uncertainty.

3. **Embrace complementary truths:** Understand that truths discovered through different methods can coexist and enrich your overall comprehension, just as the two fish scientists' findings complemented each other. If the only truth you are after is what aligns with what you've already decided, then the truth you have will rarely grow—and the fictions you pack around that truth undoubtedly will grow.

4. **Cultivate humility in learning:** Acknowledge that your preferred method of discovering truth is not the only valid approach. Be humble in your pursuit of knowledge, recognizing the value in diverse perspectives and experiences.

5. **Never allow a difference in perspective to compromise your love for another person:** Have you ever been quick to judge a person based only on something they believe differently than you? Instead, try taking some time to really get to know someone who holds a different perspective. It doesn't have to transform your core truths or shift your belief to theirs in order for your truth, knowledge, and wisdom to grow through the experience. In so doing, your likeness to God and His attributes will increase.

The story of the fish scientists demonstrates how shocking it can be that one method for obtaining truth could be rejected so completely. Of course, what this simple parable does not address is the existence of falsehoods and deception. Navigating our information-packed world requires more delicacy than simply embracing any and all declarations as true—what a mess that would be! We need to know how to recognize and manage the clutter of misinformation so we can focus on finding and embracing truth.

Chapter 3

BOUNDARIES OF TRUTH:
WHO KNOWS WHAT FROM WHERE

There really is absolute truth—eternal truth.
One of the plagues of our day is that too few
people know where to turn for truth.

—President Russell M. Nelson

While serving as a full-time missionary in the Atlanta, Georgia, area, I was blessed to meet many wonderful people. Whether it was by knocking doors in the sweltering humidity of the Southern summer or delivering free Bibles to those who responded to ads, there were always people to meet and learn from. Even though I carried a conviction for the truthfulness of the restored gospel that I offered to share with anyone who would listen, I also developed a great love and respect for the experiences, insights, and truth often shared by those I met.

One of the more uncommon friendships I developed was with a talented minister of the Church of Christ named Tom.* In the organizational structure of the Church of Christ, congregations are led by a group of elders who sometimes may also serve as preachers. Tom was an elder and preacher in the largest Christian congregation in the city I was serving in, with nearly 2,000 members attending Sunday services. We began meeting weekly at Tom's office, and our initial meetings carried a dose of skepticism toward each other, with many questions

---

* Not his real name.

starting with "Don't you believe that . . ." or "Isn't it odd that . . . ." However, as the weeks went on, we moved past these and began to have truly productive and enlightening discussions. I recall Tom helping me with how to explain the importance of baptism by immersion—a belief we held in common—to a potential convert my companion and I had been teaching. His insights were phenomenal!

At Tom's invitation, my companion and I attended one of their Sunday services. I found the sermon to be inspiring and the members kind. We reciprocated with an invitation for him to attend our worship services, but his Sunday duties and our meeting time made this challenging. As early October approached, we had the perfect idea: Tom could attend a Saturday session of general conference! We'd been having some very active discussions about prophets and their role in God's work throughout time, so the opportunity to have Tom listen to modern-day prophets was very exciting. He agreed to attend.

Before continuing this story, I need to drag you back to the late 1990s. The internet was limited and sluggish. Broadcasting of general conference to TV channels outside of Utah was very rare and usually only to special channels available with an expensive cable package.† If you wanted to watch general conference live, you had to go to your local meetinghouse that was equipped with a satellite dish for picking up the broadcast and playing it in the chapel. If you were watching conference as it was happening, then you were in a chapel or in the Intermountain West, where it was carried on local TV stations.

Back to the story. Tom agreed to attend general conference and met us at the church for the Saturday morning session. Throughout the meeting, I hung on every word, processing and interpreting it to the best of my ability as if I were Tom. My mind was filled with silent cheers

---

† "Cable" is what we called an advanced TV service that gave you access to lots of channels. If you didn't have cable TV, then you only picked up the local channels available via an antenna on your house.

of *good point* and *that was powerful*, and my confidence grew that Tom must be loving the session. I was also thrilled that President Gordon B. Hinckley had opened the conference with inspiring remarks, and that one of the talks was focused on the blessings of modern prophets.

When the session ended, we walked with Tom out to his car. I broke the silence of a nearly empty parking lot by asking, "What'd you think?" He stopped walking, turned to face us, and with a furrowed brow asked, "Let me get this straight. You've told me that the Hinckley gentleman who spoke is held as a prophet, right? That he speaks for God right now, providing instruction in the same manner as Moses, Noah, or Isaiah?"

While it was clear he was perplexed, I still felt encouraged by his thought process and answered, "Yes, that's right."

"Well, I'm confused, then. You see, if I believed *that*, then you couldn't keep me away from listening to every word he said the moment it left his lips! I would be at his feet, eager to learn and respond to whatever message the Lord was delivering. And yet, there were maybe ten people in that chapel out of the hundreds of members you say are in this area! *I wonder if your people really understand what they believe.*"

We were stunned. In all our excitement about having Tom attend the session, it hadn't occurred to us that the sparse attendance sent a confusing message. I stumbled through excuses about how many of the members would read the messages when they came out in the Church magazines the next month, but there was really no sufficient explanation for the incongruity of what he had observed.

In the years since that experience, I have often pondered Tom's comment. *Do we really understand what it is we believe?* Among the many lessons I've extracted from this story, one is that the reality of truth is not necessarily matched by expected evidence. To Tom, the evidence of a living prophet would be widespread attention to his teachings, at the very least by the few hundred members of the Church in the local congregation who profess to believe he is a prophet. While I chose to give members the benefit of the doubt, Tom used the observation to amplify his doubt in the truthfulness of our message—if the members didn't really act on what they professed to believe, it must be because the thing they believe isn't true.

Does whether or not someone believes something affect its truthfulness? Do all empirical evidences (observations) have to match up with expectation in order for something to be true? If so, who sets these expectations? Answers to these questions may be simple, but remembering and living the associated principles can be challenging, particularly when faced with the expansive breadth of information in the world, sourced from science to spirituality.

In reality, the extent to which something is believed or embraced by those who believe it has no bearing on whether it is true. A common fallacy known as the "illusion of truth" suggests that the more we are exposed to something, the more likely we are to consider it true based on nothing more than familiarity.[*] Conversely, when we learn of something wholly different from what we're used to, our instinct will be to reject it as false because of the lack of familiarity. These fallacies[†] are a subset of many we may fall prey to as we're required to quickly decide where we stand on the many topics confronting us every day.

Our world is a broad landscape of information that must be navigated

---

[*] Despite the illusion of truth (or "illusory truth") effect, it has been found that when individuals believe the repeated falsehoods, they still retain an underlying awareness of what is actually true. This suggests that while repetition can make false statements feel more believable, it does not necessarily erase one's actual knowledge of the truth. See Lisa K. Fazio, "Repetition Increases Perceived Truth Even for Known Falsehoods," *Collabra: Psychology* (2020) 6(1):38; available at https://online.ucpress.edu/collabra /article/6/1/38/114468/Repetition-Increases-Perceived-Truth-Even-for; accessed 6 November 2024.

[†] For a review of many common logical fallacies, along with helpful guidance on how to avoid them, see Hershey H. Friedman and Leon Kaganovskiy, "Logical Fallacies: How They Undermine Critical Thinking and How to Avoid Them," *SSRN*, 10 June 2024; available at https://ssrn.com/abstract=4794200; accessed 6 November 2024.

for its truthfulness by factors including what is believed, who believes it (e.g., their character, your relationship to them), and the evidence of this belief. Despite the endless variation in vantage points across this landscape, there is in fact an actual, absolute truth to all things. It's the truth that is a "knowledge of things as they are, and as they were, and as they are to come" (Doctrine and Covenants 93:24). This absolute truth has truthfulness independent of its popularity. As reviewed in the previous chapter, this truth can come from any number of sources, which we will broadly classify as scientific and gospel for the simplicity of creating a diagram.

Truth Boundaries Diagram

It can be helpful to visualize the landscape of information—fact and fiction—that makes up the world around us. My hope is that understanding the various sources of information within the context of absolute truth will aid in navigating the noisy environment we live in each day. With this goal in mind, let's create a diagram to help visualize the vast array of information in the world and how it compares to the absolute truth.

God is omniscient, knowing all truth, so our diagram will begin with a central point that represents God (see Figure 5). This dot representing God is the center of a perfect circle, which represents the whole truth. Note the circle is not yet shown in Figure 5. The "whole truth" circle is absolute truth about all things (see Doctrine and Covenants 93:24). From this circle, we carve out a small slice—like a sliver of pie—representing irrefutable truth, which is truth that we all share with virtually no dispute. The diagram up to this point, except for the perfect circle, is shown in Figure 5. Within this slice of irrefutable truth are facts like plants grow, the sun warms, we need air to breathe, and the Book of Mormon exists. These points are not open for debate when working from basic grounds of rational and logical thought. In a devotional given at Brigham Young University in 1977, President Spencer W. Kimball identified these as absolute or undeniable truths:

The earth is spherical. If all the four billion people in the world think it flat, they are in error. That is an absolute truth, and all the arguing in the world will not change it. Weights will not suspend themselves in the air, but when released will fall earthward. The law of gravity is an absolute truth. It never varies. Greater laws can overcome lesser ones, but that does not change their undeniable truth.[1]

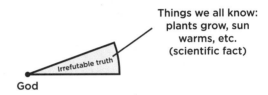

Figure 5. First step in the truth boundaries diagram. The dot represents God, who is the source of all truth, and is at the center of a perfect circle (not shown) that represents the whole truth. A small slice (like a pie slice) of the whole truth circle is shown, labeled "irrefutable truth," representing things we all know—they are undeniable or scientific fact. These include the rising of the sun, the human need for oxygen, etc.

With this initial diagram in place, let's try a little experiment. If you'd like to try this for yourself, you can either deface the page of your book or get a separate piece of paper and reproduce the dot and pie slice from Figure 5 as a starting point. Now, take a pen, pencil, or marker and place the tip at the top-right corner of the small slice that represents irrefutable truth. Here's where it gets fun. Close your eyes, take a deep breath, count to ten, and then (with your eyes still closed) try to create a perfect circle with the dot at the exact center, starting and ending from that same point. Keep your eyes closed through the entire process!

If your attempt is anything like mine, then your circle doesn't look very circular, and the dot labeled "God" is definitely not at the exact center! To see how your creation compares to a perfect circle will require the help of something like a drawing compass (we'll talk about this tool a bit later). For an example of what a blindly sketched circle looks like compared to a perfect circle with the dot at the center, see Figure 6.*

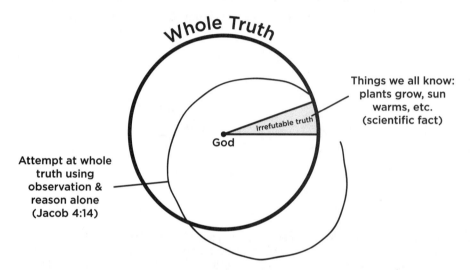

Figure 6. Next step in creating truth boundaries diagram. What is shown here is an example of the attempted sketch of a perfect "whole truth" circle after placing the tip of a pen at the top-right corner of the "irrefutable truth" slice and being blindfolded. This represents the attempt at grasping the whole truth using observation and reason (e.g., the scientific method and theory) alone. The perfect "whole truth" circle is shown for comparison, with God at the exact center as the source of all truth, "circumscribed into one great whole."

The representation of the whole truth as a circle with God at the center came to me as I studied Elder D. Todd Christofferson's inspiring talk from January of 2018 in which he taught:

> By these things, then, we know that truth exists, that it represents a fixed and immutable reality, that unaided, the quantity of

---

* There's a website where you can try to draw a perfect circle around a provided dot, and it will give you a percent accuracy. Give it a try, but make sure you close your eyes if you want to replicate this experiment! The website is https://neal.fun/perfect-circle/.

truth that mortals can discern is relatively small, that we depend on the help of divine revelation to learn "the truth of all things," and that we and God depend on truth to act and create, "otherwise there is no existence." Elsewhere we also learn that truth does not conflict with truth, but that indeed all truth may be circumscribed into one great whole.[2]

It may be a simplification to illustrate all truth as encompassed by a perfect circle, but there is much we can learn from this imagery about the landscape of truth and falsehoods in the world. One thing is for sure, the Figure 6 diagram is overly generous in representing the amount of truth we can discern as mortals, which, as Elder Christofferson states, "is relatively small."

Things "Science" Explains and Enables

The imperfect shape that was created and the process of creating it represents the temporal discoveries, experiences, and theories we may use to try and capture the whole truth. Using the vehicles of observation and reason, including gathering empirical evidence, these approaches produce a lot of accurate truth, as represented by the portion of the newly drawn shape that is within the perfect circle of whole truth. From Newton's laws of motion to Einstein's quantum phenomena, the scientific process has yielded incredible validated insights into the physical operations of our world and universe.

Discoveries, inventions, and explanations brought about through observation and reason are not limited to what we may term "hard scientific truth," but cover all fields from the "soft sciences," such as psychology and sociology, to the arts, such as music and literature. Uncovering these truths has followed a process that is similar to the blind attempt at creating the perfect circle: We start with what's known and follow the best possible process for learning more (e.g., the scientific method). This requires some assumptions and hypothesizing, testing and retesting, and an often disturbingly long list of variables and noise; but in the end, a lot of truth will be discovered—along with some falsehoods confused as truth.

I've had hundreds of people attempt this little experiment of trying to sketch the perfect circle, and something that fascinates me is that, in every instance, the shape they create encompasses the dot representing God within it (that is, every attempt at creating the circle results in some shape that contains the dot within it). To me, this symbolizes that there is always room for God in science or any other path taken to uncover truth. Excluding the presence and central role of a Supreme Being in our picture of truth must be done intentionally—either by willful scribbling around the dot or by using an eraser. As an early pioneer of transplant surgery, Dr. Joseph E. Murray, said:

> Science and religion are two sides of the same coin, and they complement each other. Science is a way of understanding the natural world, while religion provides a moral framework and a sense of purpose. Together, they can help us achieve a deeper understanding of our existence and our place in the universe.[3]

Without including God in our picture of truth about the universe, the depth of what we know is compromised, just as it is without science or human experience, and so forth.

Things "Science" Will Never Explain

Now let's dig into some of the other features of our imperfect circle, representing the attempt to capture all truth using observation and reason. Notice that there's a portion of the perfect circle of whole truth that is not encompassed by the imperfect shape. This is highlighted in Figure 7 and represents the things "science" will never explain (note, *science* is in quotes to indicate that this is not limited to scientific learning but refers to any temporal process followed in an effort to identify truth). As King Benjamin taught, "believe that man doth not comprehend all the things which the Lord can comprehend" (Mosiah 4:9). Of course, ongoing scientific studies, not to mention lived experience, continues to push this boundary further and further into the circle of whole truth—but it will never encompass it entirely. There are far too many unanswerable questions that cannot be solved using empirical methods—which focus primarily on uncovering "how" things function in the physical realm* but cannot approach the "why" behind how things transpire in our lives, the source and connection between emotions, morality, memories, and decision-making, when life begins and ends, and so forth. As scientist Dr. Scott R. Frazer described:

> Science can teach us a lot of things, but it can't teach us everything. Science cannot answer questions involving ethics or morality, such as what is fair, moral, or the right thing to do. Science cannot point a telescope into the heavens and detect if there is a God there. There is no instrument that can detect a spirit in your body or a meter to verify spiritual power or communication in prayer. Science cannot prove the existence of an afterlife, despite the many books written on hauntings and near-death experiences.[4]

On the flip side of this argument, I also hope it is understood that there are many things science *does* provide an understanding of—things that would not be accessible using theology alone. It comes back to the complementary nature of different paths or methodologies to discovering truth, as the parable of the fish scientists illustrated.

---

* There is an insightful discussion on this point in the article: Alicia K. Stanton, "Science and Our Search for Truth," *Ensign*, July 2016. From article: "Sister Ellen Mangrum, who studied chemical engineering at Rensselaer Polytechnic Institute in New York, USA, explains it this way: 'Science explains the how. But it stops short of explaining the why.' She adds that religion is what explains the why, such as why the earth was created and why we were put here."

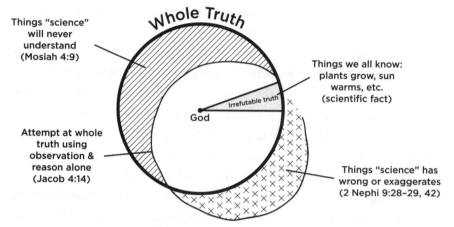

Things "science" will never understand (Mosiah 4:9)

Whole Truth

Things we all know: plants grow, sun warms, etc. (scientific fact)

Irrefutable truth

God

Attempt at whole truth using observation & reason alone (Jacob 4:14)

Things "science" has wrong or exaggerates (2 Nephi 9:28–29, 42)

Figure 7. Truth boundaries diagram. The attempt to create the perfect "whole truth" circle using observation and reason alone resulted in an imperfect circle with a region of the whole truth that "science" (or any other temporal process) will never understand and revealing a region of assumed truth that "science" has wrong. Only God knows, and can lead us to, the whole truth.

Things "Science" Gets Wrong

Let's turn our attention to the portion of the imperfect circle that extends well outside the boundary of the perfect circle of whole truth. This represents the things that scientific conclusions or human interpretations have gotten wrong. Much of this relates to attempts to fill in the gaps, whether it be about history or about a physical phenomenon—where theory or guesswork is used to piece things together in a manner that distorts the truth. Note: this is not a region of things that are *known* to be false and believed anyway; rather, it's where the facts and data received are interpreted in a way that is *un*knowingly inaccurate. Remember, the imperfect shape is created based on what is *believed* to be true given our current knowledge and understanding.

Before diving too far into this area, I want to point out something *very important*: Science as a broad discipline is not seeking to intentionally push falsehoods. Pure scientists, at their core, view this as an important value. I've known scientists from all different fields and have yet to meet anyone that was devilishly bent on promoting baseless claims and outright lies. That said, scientists are human, and there are notable instances of falsehoods being pushed in the name of supposedly supportive science. These instances are almost always fueled by the selfish ambition of an isolated scientist to achieve fame or wealth.[*] My personal experience is that the overwhelming majority of scientists are genuine in their pursuit of truth. In fact, there are major campaigns designed to weed out all forms of misinformation, whether deceitfully or unwittingly reported.[†] The point of this region of our diagram is *not* to provide a convenient place to stuff all the things you personally dislike or have decided not to believe despite the support those things have from the scientific community.

At the same time, it's reasonable to note there are many instances in which the scientific world has gotten things wrong and required revision. A few of these now-embarrassing examples which have been widely corrected include the use of bloodletting to treat illness,[‡]

---

[*] A widely publicized example was Elizabeth Holmes, who was convicted of fraud after raising more than $700 million in support of her company, Theranos, based on claims that the company had developed a technology capable of detecting numerous medical conditions from a single drop of blood. In time, it was found that the claims were exaggerated, and the technology was not able to deliver on what was promised.

[†] For example, in 2022 the National Academies of Sciences, Engineering, and Medicine in the United States formed a committee focused on "Understanding and Addressing Misinformation about Science," with the goal of improving the quality of scientific reporting at all stages, including how findings are interpreted by media and lay citizens (this is the point at which the most misinformation is generated). More information about the committee is available at https://www.nationalacademies.org/our-work/understanding-and-addressing-misinformation-about-science; accessed 6 November 2024.

[‡] An excellent discussion on this can be found in: Alicia K. Stanton, "Science and Our Search for Truth," *New Era*, July 2016; available at https://www.churchofjesuschrist.org/study/new-era/2016/07/science-and-our-search-for-truth?lang=eng; accessed 6 November 2024. In the article, the example of bloodletting is provided as an indication that "just because a belief is widely accepted or has been around for a long time doesn't necessarily mean it's true."

disregard of the role of handwashing (or hygiene in general) in stopping the spread of disease, promotion of cigarette smoking for its health benefits, and the geocentric model of the universe that taught that Earth is at the center with everything orbiting around it. As President Spencer W. Kimball taught:

> As science has expanded our understanding of the physical world, certain accepted ideas of science have had to be abandoned in the interest of truth. Some of these seeming truths were stoutly maintained for centuries. The sincere searching of science often rests only on the threshold of truth, whereas revealed facts give us certain absolute truths as a beginning point so we may come to understand the nature of man and the purpose of his life.[5]

How many other examples can you think of? Keep in mind, this region of our imperfect circle is about more than just the natural sciences. For example, there are countless instances of historical inaccuracy when events are recorded with biased, lopsided perspectives. Without additional information and the ability to determine its veracity, we are largely left to make our best educated determination about what is true. Learning certain theological truths is not exempt from this region, when we extrapolate from the core or fundamental gospel truth we've obtained and thereby extend the intended meaning of the word of God. Even without such extrapolation, we're also taught that our learning of gospel truth happens "line upon line, precept upon precept, here a little and there a little" (2 Nephi 28:30). Regardless of the topic, there are those who are "learned" yet unwittingly reliant on interpretations, information, and perspectives from this region outside the circle of whole truth. The prophet Jacob spoke of these people when he taught:

> O that cunning plan of the evil one! O the vainness, and the frailties, and the foolishness of men! When they are learned they think they are wise, and they hearken not unto the counsel of God,

for they set it aside, supposing they know of themselves, wherefore, their wisdom is foolishness and it profiteth them not. And they shall perish.

But to be learned is good if they hearken unto the counsels of God. (2 Nephi 9:28–29)

Consider the descriptive words and phrases in these verses as they relate to the truth boundaries diagram in Figure 7. The striped region that extends outside of the whole truth circle might be labeled "vainness," "frailties," "foolishness," "supposing [to] know," or "hearken[ing] not unto the counsel of God" (2 Nephi 9:28). Jacob clearly had many run-ins with, and reflections about, those who push their beliefs deeply into the space outside the circle of whole truth. In his writings, years after the sermon in 2 Nephi 9, he reflects on why the Jews rejected the prophets over the years past:

But behold, the Jews were a stiffnecked people; and they despised the words of plainness, and killed the prophets, and *sought for things that they could not understand.* Wherefore, because of their *blindness*, which blindness came by looking beyond the mark, they must needs fall; for God hath taken away his plainness from them, and delivered unto them many things which they cannot understand, because they desired it. And because they desired it God hath done it, that they may stumble. (Jacob 4:14; emphasis added)

Really, the entirety of Jacob 4 is worth a review based on the truth boundaries diagram laid out in Figure 7. In a manner far more eloquent and concise, Jacob provides clarity regarding the source of truth and how to avoid the pitfalls of excessive dependence on our own intellect or influences. Consider a few more excerpts from his teachings:

Behold, great and marvelous are the works of the Lord. How unsearchable are the depths of the mysteries of him; and *it is impossible that man should find out all his ways.* And no man knoweth of his ways save it be revealed unto him; wherefore, brethren, despise not the revelations of God. . . .

Wherefore, brethren, seek not to counsel the Lord, but to take counsel from his hand. . . .

Behold, my brethren, he that prophesieth, let him prophesy to the understanding of men; for *the Spirit speaketh the truth and lieth not.* Wherefore, it speaketh of things as they really are, and of things as they really will be; wherefore, these things are manifested unto us plainly, for the salvation of our souls. But behold, we are not witnesses alone in these things; for God also spake them unto prophets of old. (Jacob 4:8, 10, 13; emphasis added)

Those who are willing to seek learning while continuing to hearken to the counsels of God will have the Spirit of truth to be their guide, illuminating the landscape of information in a manner that can identify falsehood and keep one's beliefs contained within the "whole truth" circle. I don't want to oversimplify the utility of the Spirit in navigating the confusing mess that is this expansive region of falsehoods continually generated and amplified by the world; rather, one of the primary goals of this book is to indicate why the fundamental tools of the gospel of Jesus Christ provide a stable means for navigating the information jungle in which we live.

Core Truths

As we navigate the overwhelming landscape of information in search of what is true, we must appreciate the relative importance of the truths we embrace. As noted earlier, the region of Figure 7 filled with x's, which we labeled as things "science" (generally referring to any person's observation and reason) has wrong or exaggerates, should constantly have its boundary pushed back toward the whole truth circle. As new data is collected, scientific theories are revised, and understanding improves. The same should be true for all that we hold as truth, recognizing that we do not have a perfect knowledge of all things—with one exception: the core truths of the gospel of Jesus Christ. As Elder Dieter F. Uchtdorf put into perspective:

> The restored gospel of Jesus Christ, as the Prophet Joseph Smith taught, "embrace[s] all, and every item of truth." But that doesn't mean that all truth is of equal value. Some truths are core, essential, at the root of our faith. Others are appendages or branches—valuable, but only when they are connected to the fundamentals.[6]

Core truths of the gospel include the existence of God and His attributes of justice, mercy, long-suffering, and love. The Atonement of Jesus Christ, including the enabling power of His grace and the invitation for all to partake of His goodness, are also core truths. Additionally, the incomparable "two great commandments" of loving God and loving others (see Matthew 22:36–40) are central doctrines or truths. Any truth that brings us to God and helps us understand Him or enables us to serve Him is at the core of the whole truth circle, as depicted in Figure 8. Of these truths, we are given the promise of obtaining a perfect knowledge (see Alma 32:34)—not a knowledge that eliminates the need for ongoing faith (see Alma 32:35–36), but a knowledge that secures these truths as incontrovertible, unchanging, and fundamental—hence, core truths.

For any who may struggle with a certain policy or practice in the Church, keep in mind that these are separate from the core truth or doctrine of the gospel. As has been taught repeatedly by latter-day prophets and Church leaders, doctrine is eternal and unchanging, while policies, programs, and procedures can be adapted to apply doctrine, develop practices, and implement strategies to meet the needs of the Church and its members.* Elder John C. Pingree Jr. explained this well:

---

* See, for example: John C. Pingree Jr., "Eternal Truth," *Liahona,* November 2023; Dieter F. Uchtdorf, "Come, Join with Us," *Ensign,* November 2013; "What's the difference between Church policy and doctrine?" *ChurchofJesusChrist.org* (website), 17 May

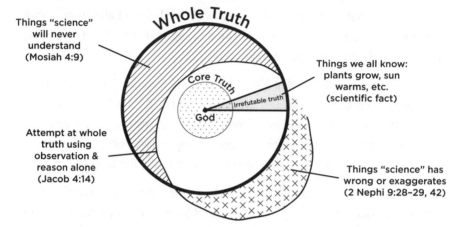

Figure 8. Final truth boundaries diagram. The attempt to create the perfect "whole truth" circle using observation and reason alone resulted in an imperfect circle with a region of the whole truth that "science" will never understand and revealing a region of assumed truth that "science" has wrong. Only God knows, and can lead us to, the whole truth. Centered around, and emanating from, God is the core truth of the gospel of Jesus Christ, which should never be compromised in our search for more truth.

When seeking truth, it helps to understand the difference between doctrine and policy. Doctrine refers to eternal truths, such as the nature of the Godhead, the plan of salvation, and Jesus Christ's atoning sacrifice. Policy is the application of doctrine based on current circumstances. Policy helps us administer the Church in an orderly way.

While doctrine never changes, policy adjusts from time to time. The Lord works through His prophets to uphold His doctrine and to modify Church policies according to the needs of His children.

Unfortunately, we sometimes confuse policy with doctrine. If we do not understand the difference, we risk becoming disillusioned when policies change and may even begin to question God's wisdom or the revelatory role of prophets.[7]

2021; available at https://www.churchofjesuschrist.org/inspiration/whats-the-difference-between-church-policy-and-doctrine?lang=eng.

This message is of overarching importance in the truth boundaries diagram: do not throw the baby (core truths) out with the bathwater (revisions to your truth boundary)! As you wrestle with any policy or practice in the Church or with aspects of seeking truth across various topics in the world, do not allow these to penetrate the core, fundamental truths of the gospel of Jesus Christ. We will explore how you establish this core truth within your own truth boundaries diagram in the coming chapters of this book.

How Do We Navigate this Landscape?

As we conclude the development of what I call the truth boundaries diagram, I hope the picture doesn't seem too bleak. Much of the diagram highlights regions of danger in the information surrounding us—from outright falsehoods embraced by those who may be "learned" and seem "wise," to vast areas of truth that remain completely inaccessible using only the tools of observation and reason (e.g., the scientific method). But we should keep Mormon's counsel to his son, Moroni, in mind:

> My son, be faithful in Christ; and may not the things which I have written grieve thee, to weigh thee down unto death; but may Christ lift thee up, and may his sufferings and death, and the showing his body unto our fathers, and his mercy and long-suffering, and the hope of his glory and of eternal life, rest in your mind forever. (Moroni 9:25)

It's worth considering the glorious truths we have available to us, particularly in our day! There are incredible scientific discoveries, inspiring and ingenious creations of art and music, and a greater collection of lived experience and learning than has ever existed on this planet. All of these contribute to the truth within our reach to learn and believe in. However, without humble and faithful reliance on the one source of all truth, even our omniscient God, we can never come to know all things (see Doctrine and Covenants 88:67). It's imperative to keep God at the center of our truth, for if He is not at the center, then what is there instead? Even a small shift in our recognition of, and dependence on, God can have sizable implications to what we hold as truth. In the following chapters, we'll explore the paths we can walk to navigate this world of information deluge in a manner that leads us to the whole truth, which can only come from God.

Applying the Principles

1. **Recognize the limits of human understanding:** Remember that no single human perspective can encompass the whole truth. Be aware there are boundaries to your knowledge and remain open to divine guidance and ongoing learning, a little at a time (see 2 Nephi 28:30).

2. **Seek to establish and never compromise core truth:** While scientific and logical findings of what is true may require revision or correction over time as new information is received and verified, core truths are eternal and unchanging. These include the plan of salvation, the Atonement of Jesus Christ, and God's love for all His children. Take some time to identify and fortify your core of gospel truths. Meanwhile, be open to expanding your understanding through further revelation and learning, remaining centered on God.

3. **Be sure to understand what you believe:** As I learned from my experience with Tom, my minister friend from the Church of Christ, it's important that we understand the import of what we believe. It may be helpful to take an inventory of the most important core truths of the gospel in your life. Are you living in a way that is consistent with these beliefs? Later, we will modify this statement from "understanding what you believe" to "believing what you know."

4. **Keep God at the center of your truth:** Regardless of the topic or method by which you're pursuing truth, never compromise keeping

God at the center. Recent guidance from the Church regarding seeking answers to questions is to "Center Your Life on Jesus Christ," holding onto what you know, distinguishing core truths, and choosing to walk by faith.[8] What can you do to re-center your life and pursuit of truth on Christ, regardless of the topic?

5. **Beware of falsehoods:** Be cautious of information that may appear true but compromises *core* fundamental gospel truth. Meanwhile, recognize the role of revision to our truth boundaries as we gain more understanding through our openness to learning and our dependence on God; it's certainly not just science that requires occasional revision! Our understanding of gospel truths should be expanding as well. Discernment, guided by the Holy Spirit, is crucial in navigating the complex landscape of information.

It's clear that I love diagrams. While they help me with visualizing the landscape of information and how it relates to real truth, that doesn't mean they capture everything. You may have a far better way to visualize this or, more importantly, to live it! What matters most here is a recognition that God is the source of all truth, and that our dependence on Him, walking on His path, is what will most precisely lead us to comprehending more and more truth and filtering out falsehoods. What exactly is that path and how do we walk it? We'll explore this in the next chapter, taking the truth boundaries diagram one step further.

Chapter 4

A STRAIGHT PATH THAT IS ROUND

Are you seeking to cut through all the cunning and the snares and the wiles of the devil so prevalent in the philosophies of our day? Do you desire to disperse the clouds of confusion caused by an overabundance of information in order to focus more singularly on the covenant path? Please try the virtue of the word of God.

—Elder Mark D. Eddy

When I was thirteen years old, there were few things I enjoyed more than camping with my scout troop. I grew up in a family that did not really travel for vacations, so the monthly outings to the mountains of Arizona to escape the often-oppressive heat of the Phoenix valley were highlights for me. Bless the leaders who sacrificed so much time and resources to make these campouts happen—they have had a lasting impact! One such trip was to a campsite located on Mount Ord, just an hour and a half from where we lived in East Phoenix.

The camping area was only a short hike away from the 7,128-foot peak of Mount Ord, which boasted an impressive collection of communication towers. After a typical evening of setting up camp, playing capture the flag, and gathering around the campfire, we retired to our tents. The next morning, the leaders hiked with us to the summit, where we climbed one of the communication towers for an incredible view from the peak. When we returned to the campsite, the leaders could tell we still had energy to burn, so they made us a deal: If we packed everything up within thirty minutes and then hiked down the mountain (about six miles), we would stop at Bushnell Tanks—a much-loved swimming spot—on the way home. This idea was very well received, so we packed quickly and were about to set out when our scoutmaster stopped us.

"Here's the deal," he said. "All you have to do is follow the road down. There are some smaller trails and other turnoffs along the way, but do *not* take them! If you just stay on the main dirt road, it will lead you all the way down to the highway—that's where we'll pick you up in the Suburban."

"Wait, you're not hiking with us?" we protested. It hadn't quite registered in our young brains that the vehicle would also need to get down the mountain.

"No, but you'll be just fine if you stay on the main road. We'll be waiting for you at the end."

With that, our troop of six boys, all twelve or thirteen years old, set off down the road. We started out at a run with the misguided idea that we could beat the leaders down the mountain. That lasted about a hundred yards, after which we slowed our pace and devolved into the expected behavior of kicking and throwing rocks and grumbling about how long the trek down was. At some point, the leaders passed us in the Suburban with shouts of, "You're doing great! Probably halfway there!"

The further we got down the mountain, the better our visibility became as ponderosa pines gave way to the more open desert landscape. Eventually, we rounded a bend in the road and could actually see the highway in the far-off distance. The road we were on wound in and out of view, snaking its way down the mountain in what seemed like a hundred-mile stretch. To our right, we noticed a trail branching off the road, taking what appeared to be a more direct path that reconnected with the main road farther down—a shortcut! While we couldn't see the full path of this shortcut, we were all convinced it would be faster and thus give us more time for swimming at the tanks!

As we started down the shortcut path, one of the boys said, "Aren't we supposed to stay on the main road?" This conscience-like reminder of our leaders' instructions was received with moaning, some dust-kicking, and name-calling. I'm ashamed to say that I don't remember who gave the reminder—other than that it wasn't me. In fact, I was the senior patrol leader and had the responsibility of taking the lead. I quieted the boys down so I could say, "It's just a shortcut—we'll be back on the main road in no time!"

I'm not sure how far we made it on this trail, but it took a dip down into the desert—part of the path we hadn't been able to see from the main road—and we started to get a little lost. Suddenly, gunshots echoed off the mountain backdrop: *crack, crack, crack*! One of the boys screamed (I'm *almost* certain it wasn't me!), and we all dramatically took cover behind some rocks and cacti. Were we being shot at? Our scout shirts were rather deer-colored. Maybe we were caught in the crossfire? In our young minds, we'd wandered into an active shooting range where we were potential targets!

We hunkered down in that desert valley for at least thirty minutes. Occasionally, our chatter would be interrupted by another volley of *crack, crack, crack* echoing off the mountain. Finally, we determined we'd make a run for it back the way we came (we'd managed to locate our original trail at that point). It must have been quite the sight with six boys ducking down, possibly screaming, and running as fast as we could back up the trail to the main road.

When we reached the road, we found one of our leaders running toward us. He was red-faced and out of breath, barely producing enough air to stumble out, "What . . . were . . . you . . . thinking?" We were all ashamed, especially me. I was supposed to have led these boys as instructed. I'd let my leaders down and, by virtue of my actions, let the other boys down as well.

Once he caught his breath, our leader explained that there were several shooting ranges throughout that valley, along with some active deer hunting. It wasn't necessarily that he thought we were in grave danger of being mistaken for bucks that made him upset, but that we'd gone missing and he couldn't find us. It turns out that they'd parked the Suburban just around the next bend in the main road from where we veered off onto our shortcut. They wanted to surprise us by shaving the last mile or two off our hike. If we'd just stayed the course, as instructed, we would have reached them within minutes and been off to the swimming hole.

That ride home was the quietest of any I've ever been on. As we passed the sign for Bushnell Tanks, our would-be prize for the long hike down the mountain, every head in the truck turned to look longingly. Well, every head but two—our leaders stared straight down the highway.

The Covenant Path

Amid all the noise and distraction in the world today, there's a clearly demarcated path laid before us: the covenant path. The gate by which we entered this path is "repentance and baptism" (2 Nephi 31:17), which put us on "this strait and narrow path which leads to eternal life" (2 Nephi 31:18).

> And now, my beloved brethren, after ye have gotten into this strait and narrow path, I would ask if all is done? Behold, I say unto you, Nay; for ye have not come thus far save it were by the word of Christ with unshaken faith in him, relying wholly upon the merits of him who is mighty to save. (2 Nephi 31:19)

I've come to the realization that staying on the covenant path is *simple*, but it's not *easy*. As was the case with my scout troop staying on the well-marked road as we hiked down the mountain—it wasn't complicated to distinguish the road we'd been instructed to stay on from the various trails that branched off. The difficulty was in staying focused on what mattered and not allowing the distractions of other options or opportunities to entice us off the path. Thinking back on that experience and the feelings of fear, anxiety, and uncertainty that filled my young mind when we'd intentionally veered off the path, I feel the power of President Russell M. Nelson's pleading words when he said the following to the youth of the Church:

> "Please do not stay off the covenant path one more minute. . . . Please come back through true repentance, now. We need you with us in this youth battalion of the Lord. It just won't be the same without you!"[1]

You may be thinking this little analogy of my scout troop departing from the clearly marked road is an oversimplification of the various pressures and obstacles faced on the actual covenant path we walk in life. I am certainly not oblivious to these and know they come from all facets of life, including within the Church itself. We will address these in the next chapters of this book. First, we need to clarify a couple scriptures about paths that may seem at odds with each other and see how this all relates back to the truth boundaries diagram from Chapter 3.

A Straight Path That Is Round?

I'm an engineer by education and a scientist by trade, so scriptures that use descriptive language about geometry instantly capture my attention. There are two phrases from scripture that have geometric terminology that have historically felt at odds to me. You're likely familiar with each of them individually, but I wonder if you've considered them collectively. Here they are from a couple of representative verses:

> For I perceive that ye are in the paths of righteousness; I perceive that ye are in the path which leads to the kingdom of God;

yea, I perceive that ye are making *his paths straight.* (Alma 7:19; emphasis added)

Listen to the voice of the Lord your God, even Alpha and Omega, the beginning and the end, *whose course is one eternal round,* the same today as yesterday, and forever. (Doctrine and Covenants 35:1; emphasis added)

Here's my question: How can a path be straight *and* round? I can appreciate that these phrases may not be intended as literal and can be used to teach several things about the Lord and His ways. But the need for reconciling these concepts hit me hard when I realized they're even brought *together* in some verses, such as:

For God doth not walk in crooked paths, neither doth he turn to the right hand nor to the left, neither doth he vary from that which he hath said, therefore *his paths are straight, and his course is one eternal round.* (Doctrine and Covenants 3:2; emphasis added; see also Alma 37:12)

Geometry to the Rescue!

To reconcile these seemingly divergent concepts—that the Lord's path is both straight *and* one eternal round—we'll turn to geometry. If you hate geometry, you certainly can skip this discussion and move on to the next section.

Let's start by considering how we physically move in this world. If you're standing on flat ground, you can move left or right, forward or backward; we could more technically label these options as north, south, east, and west. You could also jump in the air (a minor increment for some of us, but more significant for others!) and thus move up or down; again, more technically we could say you change altitude, also achievable by climbing. Geometrically, we can describe anywhere we might be in our navigable three-dimensional space using the Cartesian coordinate system, as shown in Figure 9A. In this coordinate system, we use x, y, and z to describe the three dimensions of movement.

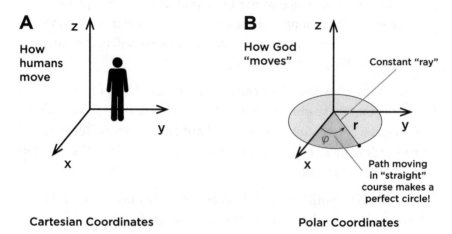

Cartesian Coordinates   **Polar Coordinates**

Figure 9. How to achieve a straight path that is round. **A:** Humans live and move in a Cartesian coordinate system, where any location can be described by three coordinates: x, y, and z. **B:** Three-dimensional space described by polar coordinates (a distance and two angles, with only one angle shown), which is one way of thinking about how God "moves." In polar coordinates, a ray (r) extends from the origin and when swept around in a straight path by an angle (φ) forms a perfect circle.

In the Cartesian coordinate system, there is no way for a straight path to generate something that is round, so describing how God "walks" (see Doctrine and Covenants 3:2) will require a different type of coordinate setup. As shown in Figure 9B, the *polar* coordinate system is still three-dimensional, but you define a specific position based on a distance from the origin (this distance is called a "ray," or r) and the tilt or angles the ray has from the origin (one of those angles is phi, labeled as φ). In these polar coordinates, if you have a fixed ray and you then sweep it on a straight path based on the angle φ all the way around (360 degrees), you will have created a perfect circle. In other words, a fixed ray r moving on a straight path φ creates a perfect round.

Now we can connect this geometric picture to the truth boundaries diagram from Chapter 3 (see Figure 10). Let's take the ray to be the word of God, which is a wonderful correlation because a "ray" calls to mind light, and there is a connection between light and truth (see Doctrine and Covenants 84:45; 88:6). We learn elsewhere that "holding fast" to the word of God and continuing on a "strait and narrow path" leads to the tree representing the love of God (see 1 Nephi 8, 11, 15). So, keeping God at the center (origin) and holding fast to the word of God (the fixed ray), we move straight forward on the covenant path (sweeping the angle φ), which will lead us to all truth (perfect round or circle).

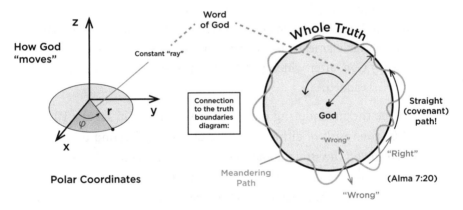

Figure 10. Connecting to the truth boundaries diagram. From Chapter 3, the truth boundaries diagram includes a perfect circle representing the whole truth, with God at the center or origin. If the ray is the word of God, then holding fast to it and moving in a straight path (by sweeping the angle φ), without veering will lead to a perfect circle—the eternal round that represents God's course. If we diminish or move beyond the word of God, we depart from the covenant path and create a meandering path of partial truth and some falsehoods.

To hold fast to the word of God means we do not toss part of it out, nor do we push beyond its boundary. This doesn't mean the word of God is not continuing to flow and bring us more and more truth—it most certainly does this as we move forward along the covenant path, sweeping the word of God to form more and more of the perfect "whole truth" circle! To move along the covenant path is to move with God on a path to "comprehend[ing] all things" because we are singularly focused on Him (Doctrine and Covenants 88:67–68). Consider Alma's teaching about the path we walk with God:

> I perceive that it has been made known unto you, by the testimony of his word, that *he cannot walk in crooked paths*; neither doth he vary from that which he hath said; neither hath he a shadow of turning from the right to the left, or from that which is right to that which is wrong; therefore, his course is one eternal round. . . .
>
> And now my beloved brethren, I have said these things unto you that I might awaken you to a sense of your duty to God, that ye may walk blameless before him, that ye may *walk after the holy order of God*, after which ye have been received. (Alma 7:20, 22; emphasis added)

Notice the meandering path that is illustrated in Figure 10. This would be the result of either rejecting or moving beyond the word of God, veering off the straight and narrow covenant path and thus missing out on some truths and embracing some falsehoods. In reality, as we stay on the covenant path, which means holding fast to the word of God without variance, we are promised that the "temptations and the fiery darts of the adversary" will not be able to "overpower [us] unto blindness, to lead [us] away to destruction" (1 Nephi 15:24). Elder D. Todd Christofferson commented on the protections and importance of staying on the covenant path in his talk, "Why the Covenant Path," where he taught:

> Too often our problems or challenges are self-inflicted, the result of poor choices, or, we could say, the result of "unforced errors." When we are diligently pursuing the covenant path, we quite naturally avoid many "unforced errors." We sidestep the various

forms of addiction. We do not fall into the ditch of dishonest conduct. We cross over the abyss of immorality and infidelity. We bypass the people and things that, even if popular, would jeopardize our physical and spiritual well-being. We avoid the choices that harm or disadvantage others and instead acquire the habits of self-discipline and service.

Elder J. Golden Kimball is purported to have said, "I may not have [always] walked the straight and narrow, but I [try] to cross it as often as I [can]." In a more serious moment, I am sure Brother Kimball would agree that staying on, not just crossing, the covenant path is our greatest hope for avoiding *avoidable* misery on the one hand and successfully dealing with the *unavoidable* woes of life on the other.[2]

Each of us is walking our own unique path in life, generating our own truth boundaries diagram. If we hold fast to the word of God as we walk this path, we can avoid "turning from the right to the left, or from that which is right to that which is wrong" (Alma 7:20). This is true for all methods we pursue for finding truth.

The Compass

We can now see how moving straight along the covenant path, holding fast to the word of God, leads us to all truth and protects us from many problems and challenges. There's one further analogy we can make here based on a simple instrument you likely used in elementary school: a drawing compass, also called a pair of compasses. This compass is used to create circles, and is composed of two arms connected at a hinge that can set the arms to a certain distance apart. One of the arms has a pencil on the end and the other a point or needle. By placing the needle at the point where the center of a circle is to be scribed and setting the distance between the arms to the desired radius, the compass can be rotated with the pencil arm on the paper to create a perfect circle.

What I love about this tool for creating circles is that there is another tool in the scriptures referred to as a compass or "director": the Liahona (Alma 37:38), which was "a ball of curious workmanship . . . within the ball were two spindles; and the one pointed the way whither we should go into the wilderness" (1 Nephi 16:10). While the Liahona makes its appearance as a guiding tool for Lehi and his family in 1 Nephi 16, one of the more elaborate descriptions of its use is found in Alma 37:38–45. Across these verses, I will point out some excerpts used to describe the function of this compass that was designed to lead the Nephites on their true path (that is, the path to truth):

> It was prepared to show unto our fathers the course which they should travel . . .
>
> . . . They were slothful, and forgot to exercise their faith and diligence . . .
>
> . . . Therefore, they . . . did not travel a direct course . . .
>
> . . . (now these things were temporal) . . . even so it is with things which are spiritual.
>
> For behold, it is as easy to give heed to the word of Christ, which will point to you a straight course to eternal bliss, as it was for our fathers to give heed to this compass, which would point unto them a straight course to the promised land.
>
> And now I say, is there not a type in this thing? For just as surely as this director did bring our fathers, by following its course, to the promised land, shall the words of Christ, if we follow their course, carry us beyond this vale of sorrow into a far better land of promise. (Alma 37:39, 41–45)

Just as illustrated in our geometry example of Figures 9 and 10, and in Lehi's dream, and with the Liahona—it's the word of God and pressing forward on the covenant path that can provide protection, comfort, and truth in all things.

Why Bother Making Sense Out of This?

I imagine you may be wondering why we bothered going through all of this. I mean, what do geometry and compasses have to do with the actual walking of the covenant path in life? How does envisioning the Lord's path being straight while scribing into a perfect circle really help navigate the chaotic world our path leads through?

The answer is found in what this teaches us about our Heavenly Father. Regardless of all the noise and distraction in the world, the enticements and pressures that we face, and the endless options we're confronted with, His paths are straight—and following them will lead us in an "eternal round" representative of our understanding all truth (see Doctrine and Covenants 88:67). And it's not just about the surety of His promises to us, but also about what this entire discussion about paths and circles teaches us about our Lord and Savior, Jesus Christ. We can put our trust in the following assurances:

> [God] cannot walk in crooked paths; neither doth he vary from that which he hath said; neither hath he a shadow of turning from the right to the left, or from that which is right to that which is wrong; therefore, his course is one eternal round. (Alma 7:20)
>
> For he that diligently seeketh shall find; and the mysteries of God shall be unfolded unto them, by the power of the Holy Ghost, as well in these times as in times of old, and as well in times of old as in times to come; wherefore, the course of the Lord is one eternal round. (1 Nephi 10:19)

The second of these two verses comes right before Nephi describes receiving one of the most glorious visions in all of scripture, where he comes to understand truth about things to come that could not have been accessed in any other way. And what did Nephi want us to know about this truth? That it was available to each one of us, just as it was "in times of old" (1 Nephi 10:19).

The other takeaway here is that you cannot find truth without taking steps. The circle of truth will never form, your understanding cannot be increased or promised blessings received, if you are not moving forward. As President Nelson has often said, "The Lord loves effort."[3] Without our effort, belief never turns to faith, faith never turns to knowledge, and our part of the covenant falls dormant. In the October 2022 general conference, Sister Michelle D. Craig of the Young Women General Presidency shared a touching story that exemplifies this reality. When her family was getting new carpet in their house, Sister Craig's brothers played a prank on her little seven-year-old sister, Emily. While Emily slept, the brothers removed the carpet and all her belongings from her room and left a note saying the family had moved. When she awoke the next morning to an empty room and the note, Emily was crushed, thinking her family really had left her behind. The family grew concerned when she didn't come to breakfast, so the brothers went to her room and found her in the closet, crying. Sister Craig shared:

> My sister made an assumption based on what she saw, but it wasn't a reflection of the way things actually were. Isn't it interesting that we, like Emily, can become so weighed down in sadness or hurt or discouragement or worry or loneliness or anger or frustration that it doesn't even occur to us to simply do something, to open the door, to act with faith in Jesus Christ?[4]

Without our effort, we offer little for God to work with on the altar of truth. As we press forward, acting and seeking truth with faith in Jesus Christ, He can provide us with greater light and comprehension of all things around us.

Applying the Principles

1. **Stay on the covenant path:** Just as the straight path in the polar coordinates analogy leads to a perfect circle, diligently following the covenant path will lead you to greater truth and spiritual safety. This requires holding to the word of God while actively and patiently stepping forward to receive greater and greater comprehension of the whole truth. When confronted with new information, evaluate it with openness while holding fast to the word of God.

2. **Avoid distractions and shortcuts:** Life will present many diversions that seem easier or more appealing. Resist the temptation to stray from the covenant path, understanding that these detours can lead to confusion and spiritual danger, ultimately robbing you of your long-term goal. It's not worth halting your progress on the covenant path to stop and consider the enticing neon billboards that seek to amplify your own sense of knowledge or power—keep moving forward!

3. **Trust in the Lord's unchanging nature:** The Lord's path is both straight and eternal. Trust that as you adhere to His word and covenants, you are progressing toward a comprehensive understanding of truth on His timetable. His guidance may be specific to each person's circumstances, but the constancy and surety of His promises can be trusted as unchanging and timeless—following Him will lead to greater joy, light, and truth.

4. **Apply effort and faith:** Progress on the covenant path requires consistent effort. Engage actively in gospel learning, knowing that the Lord values your effort and will guide you toward the truth. Remember, the purpose of the covenants we make is to help us become more like God, able to receive all that He has (see Doctrine and Covenants 88:32–33).

As exemplified by my camping trip as a young boy when we experienced the consequences of knowingly departing from the instructed roadway, it's imperative that we hold to the word of God to stay on the covenant path. Remember, it's our effort that the Lord loves; of course there will be need for daily repentance along the way, but so long as we are pressing forward, striving to hold to the word of God, we will find protection and blessings in our search for more truth. As the quote from Elder Mark D. Eddy at the beginning of this chapter reminds us, if we want to cut through the snares of the devil and "disperse the clouds of confusion caused by an overabundance of information," we must "try the virtue of the word of God."[5] Holding fast to His word and pressing forward will lead us to all truth.

Chapter 5

THE PARABLE OF THE BRIDGE

We will never regret being too kind. In God's eyes,
kindness is synonymous with greatness.
—Elder Gary B. Sabin

You learn a lot about yourself and your spouse as you raise children together. It doesn't take long for kids to figure out which parent is best to ask for money or permission to do something out of the ordinary with their friends. They quickly learn who they'd rather deliver bad news to and who's better at celebrating exciting news. In our house, they also learn which parent they'd prefer to have making their lunch.

The entire lunch-making enterprise was my wife's idea. I'm more of a "fend for yourself" type of parent—teach them to fish, as the old saying goes! But to Lianne, making lunch for the kids, even when they're in high school, is a simple way to show love and support without the fragilities other types of interactions or efforts have when kids are that age. So rather than finding myself in the awkward position of saying, "We shouldn't show so much love for our kids," I relented and have contributed to the lunch-making tradition in our home, especially since we've had high schoolers.

But not all lunches are created equal.

Don't get me wrong—I am not *intentionally* doing a poor job of preparing lunches for nefarious purposes. My standards just aren't as high as those of my wife or, apparently, our kids. However, there is one day I must admit was a failure. It's a day that now lives in infamy in our Franklin family lore.

My son Grant was in high school at the time and had taken a liking to having a couple of hard-boiled eggs in his lunch. While I was typically the lunch maker that particular school year, I went out of town for a few days, and so Lianne stepped in while I was gone. When I returned, she debriefed me on what she had been packing for our boys. She'd just finished explaining where the carton of hard-boiled eggs was in the fridge when I heard her say, ". . . and then I peel the eggs for him and put them in a zip-top bag."

"Hold on," I interrupted, "you *peel* the eggs for him? Listen, at the very least, he can peel his own eggs."

She responded calmly, noting that he didn't have much time or a convenient way to rinse off any lingering pieces of eggshell at lunch, but added, "I guess we can see how it goes tomorrow."

The next morning at 5:30 a.m., I was up and packing the lunches. I opened the fridge to pull out the eggs and thought, "Now, what was it Lianne said about where she'd put the hard-boiled eggs?" I searched and searched, finally found the egg carton, selected two eggs and dropped them in a zip-top bag (shells intact). After finishing with the rest of the lunch items, I stuffed everything into the kids' lunch bags, and off we went to seminary.

Around lunchtime that day, a text message came through on our family group chat from Grant. It said, "Remember this day as the day Dad gave me raw eggs instead of boiled." Apparently, the carton of eggs I found wasn't the only one, and I clearly should have listened more closely when my wife was telling me this very thing the night before! I felt so bad. It really wasn't my intent to cause misery. I will admit though, it didn't take very long before the remorse wore off, and I found the situation purely comical. I think it's been enough years now that Grant feels the same way . . . probably.

This experience brings a question to mind: How much can you tell by looking at an egg? Is it possible to decipher if it is raw, fertilized, soft-boiled, hard-boiled, fresh, or rotten? Not at a glance. Even briefly handling the egg doesn't tell you much more, especially if it's the variety with thicker shells. The same is true for people. How much do you *really* know about a person by looking at them? No doubt there's much assumed, but little is actually known. The same goes for when you learn just one thing about a person, such as their views on a political topic—do you suddenly know all things about them from just this one piece of information? Of course not, it'd be like saying you now know the condition of an egg because it's a solid-colored egg rather than a speckled one.

As we work our way through life, we will encounter people with wildly different views about truth than ours. Their truth boundaries diagram may encompass many beliefs outside of our own. What should we do with that? Is it possible to be protective of our own truth, particularly our core truth, while being open to hearing and engaging with those with such divergent views? To explore these questions, I'd like to share a second parable (that is, moral story).

The Parable of the Bridge

Long ago, there was a bridge that spanned a deep chasm, as shown in Figure 11. Assembled from planks and ropes, the bridge was supported by two pillars that stood strong and steadfast on either side of the chasm. The bridge provided the only path for people from the town on one side of the chasm to access a beautiful place of gathering, refuge, and peace on the other side. While not all took advantage of the opportunity to use the bridge to access the place of peace, for those who did, it was treasured.

For those who understood the vitality of the bridge, they cherished what it brought into their lives. They would adorn the bridge with decorations and carvings representing the memories, joys, hardships,

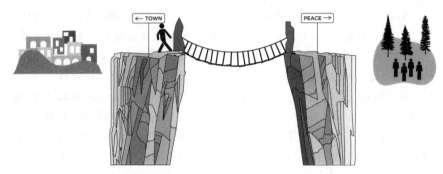

Figure 11. Parable of the bridge—part 1. A deep chasm separates a town from a place of peace. There is a bridge made from planks and ropes that crosses the chasm, supported by strong pillars on either side.

instructions, and lessons learned in their lives—their truth. Much time and energy was invested into making these displays that people so greatly prized—in many ways, the people felt like the decorations defined who they were. In time, the bridge's path reflected the history and achievements of the people. In their pursuit for perfection and recognition they had carved, woven, and adorned the planks, ropes, and pillars of the bridge, as shown in Figure 12.

One day, a master craftsman walked the bridge and noticed a slight tremor beneath his feet. Attuned to the design and feel of the bridge

Figure 12. Parable of the bridge—part 2. The people who use the bridge adorn it with decorations that represent the truth they have discovered through their experiences, studies, and accomplishments.

as he was, he felt the need to closely study the condition of the pillars. Though they were adorned with inscriptions and decorations, beneath them were cracks and deterioration, as shown in Figure 13. The many memories and reminders the people had laden the bridge with had caused them to ignore the foundational pillars. No matter how splendidly the bridge was decorated or how sturdy its planks and thick its rope, without each of the pillars firmly supporting it, the entire bridge would collapse.

Figure 13. Parable of the bridge—part 3. A master craftsman feels a tremor in the bridge and, inspecting more closely by removing superfluous decorations, finds large cracks in the supporting pillars.

The master craftsman shared his discovery with the people of the town, urging them to pay attention to the condition of the bridge's foundation (shown in Figure 14). Many of the townsfolk were too consumed with their own interests to even know the master craftsman was speaking. To most who heard the craftsman, his words seemed impossible and his warnings were dismissed. Some quickly concluded that he must not be talking about the decorations *they* loved—surely it's not *their* fault the pillars were weakening. To them, his message felt hollow, as they too greatly prized the beautifully carved planks and other decorations—surely these mattered more in supporting them as they crossed the bridge. Yet there were a few who heeded the words of the craftsman, realizing that while the embellishments were beautiful and represented things that are good, it was the pillars that ensured the bridge's stability.

Figure 14. Parable of the bridge—part 4. The master craftsman tells the people of the town about the damage to the pillars and the need to prioritize their repair. Most do not listen, many find it difficult to believe that the decorations don't matter the most, while a few take heed and seek to repair the pillars.

The few who listened followed the master craftsman to the bridge and went straight to work on fortifying the pillars. Going forward, they prioritized the pillars and their care above all other adornments or components. Yet, given the many competing forces and perspectives—will the work of only a few be enough to repair the strength of the pillars? Will the people give sufficient emphasis to the foundational structure of the bridge rather than overemphasizing the adornments that hang on it?

Meaning of the Parable

The meaning of the parable is summarized in Figure 15.

The town is a representation of our world, while the place of peace is just that, a place for peace and joy that is available now and forever. This place is accessed by crossing a bridge composed of planks and ropes, which represent the laws, duties, and commandments we receive from God. They're instrumental in making the place of peace accessible,

THE PARABLE OF THE BRIDGE

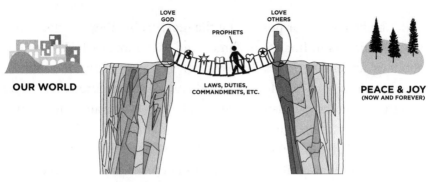

Figure 15. Parable of the bridge—part 5. Interpretation of the parable. The town is the world; the place of peace is as it sounds, a place of peace now and forever; the bridge with its planks and ropes represents the laws, duties, and commandments; the decorations represent accomplishments, things learned, or even truth gained; the master craftsman represents the prophets; and the pillars are the two great commandments.

though each person crosses the bridge by applying their weight a little differently on the various planks. The decorations adorning the bridge represent the truth obtained by the people as they have used the bridge—wonderful insights, knowledge, and understanding that has been obtained. And the master craftsman is the prophet, charged with the responsibility to instruct God's people. So what then are the pillars? Let's turn to the words of the Savior to describe these:

> Jesus said unto him, Thou shalt love the Lord thy God with all thy heart, and with all thy soul, and with all thy mind.
>
> This is the first and great commandment.
>
> And the second is like unto it, Thou shalt love thy neighbour as thyself.
>
> *On these two commandments hang all the law and the prophets.* (Matthew 22:37–40; emphasis added)

All the law and the prophets—meaning everything received, taught, expected, or required, from ordinances to service—hang on these two commandments: love God and love others. It's also instructive to consider what the pillars holding all of this together are *not.* They are not about being correct or possessing the most truth. They are not about worldly success in finance or fame. And they most certainly are not about us *demanding* others share our beliefs. Do we use whatever we've been given to show our love for God and all His children? Or do we focus more on the grandeur of what we believe is true and how it compares to others than on how we see and treat them?

Notice that you could tell little about the condition of the bridge simply by looking at it. Its cracks ran deep beneath the decorative façade of what had been embraced and celebrated as truth. Yet, it was these hidden pillars—whose integrity and care mattered most—which ensured that the place of lasting peace and joy would remain accessible.

We live in a world of blame and accusation, hatred, and vitriol. Often, harsh conclusions about a person's character and worth are reached based on limited information. But what if the primary piece of information we used to judge someone was that they are a child of God, who loves them as much as He loves us? What if we loved God enough to prioritize being peacemakers and strengthening the pillars more than decorating the planks? When all is said and done, you can strip every decorative element from the bridge, leaving it plain and bare, yet still make a secure journey to lasting peace—as long as the pillars are strong. As President Russell M. Nelson reminded us:

> The Savior's message is clear: His *true* disciples build, lift, encourage, persuade, and inspire—no matter how difficult the situation. True disciples of Jesus Christ are peacemakers.[1]

I first developed this parable of the bridge for my class at BYU Education Week in August 2023. The topic of my class was related to finding truth, and I felt compelled to share a parable that emphasized the overarching importance of loving God and loving others. About eight months later, Elder Gary E. Stevenson gave an absolutely wonderful talk in general conference titled "Bridging the Two Great Commandments," where he used the metaphor of a bridge with two strong supporting towers to illustrate the importance of the two great commandments. He didn't need a rather silly parable to drive the message home; he taught beautifully about the importance of balance between the great commandments as follows:

> Some are so focused on keeping the commandments that they show little tolerance of those they see as less righteous. Some find it difficult to love those who are choosing to live their lives outside of the covenant or even away from any religious participation.
>
> Alternatively, there are those who emphasize the importance of loving others without acknowledgment that we are all accountable to God. Some refuse entirely the notion that there is such a thing as absolute truth or right and wrong and believe that the only thing required of us is complete tolerance and acceptance of the choices of others. Either of these imbalances could cause your spiritual bridge to tip or even fall. . . .
>
> So the question for each of us is, How do we build our own bridge of faith and devotion—erecting tall bridge towers of both loving God and loving our neighbors? Well, we just start. Our initial efforts might look like a plan on the back of a napkin or an early-stage blueprint of the bridge we hope to construct. It might consist of a few realistic goals to understand the Lord's gospel more or to vow to judge others less. No one is too young or too old to begin.[2]

There is no academic degree or other requirement or qualification to take on the task of strengthening the towers (or pillars) of our own bridge of faith. Putting forth effort toward fortifying the two great commandments in our lives will ensure access to true peace and rest, no matter how much or how little we may understand about the complexities of the world around us.

Seeing Other People's Truth Boundaries

We are all constantly developing our truth boundaries diagrams to identify what we have come to know or believe to be true as we walk our path through life. Ideally, these boundaries would be formed by a perfect and unwavering adherence to the word of God while pressing forward on the covenant path. However, there must also be patience, as some truth takes time to come to us. There are also distractions and deterrents that may occasionally cause us to veer off course. By exercising humility and seeking greater learning, we can continue to grow in our understanding of what is true, correcting previously believed falsehoods and filling in gaps with previously unknown truths.

So what happens when we come across someone whose truth boundaries diagram differs from ours? This is visualized in Figure 16. If we are willing to lead with love and acknowledge that some of the other person's differences may be truths we have yet to discover, then we can maintain the strength of our pillars while also potentially expanding our truth. This doesn't mean our core truth ever needs to be compromised. You can love someone—truly love, not pity them—while recognizing what they believe as truth does not align with your core truth. Remember, if part of your core truth includes the gospel of Jesus Christ, then showing love to someone else should be a foremost priority! (See John 13:34–35; Matthew 5:43–47.) As Paul taught, if you "understand all mysteries, and all knowledge . . . and have not charity, [you are] nothing" (1 Corinthians 13:2). And the words from our loving Savior: "if ye love them which love you, what reward have ye? do not even the publicans the same? And if ye salute your brethren only, what do ye more than others?" (Matthew 5:46–47).

If you seek to love and understand those with differing views, you can learn from each other. This is illustrated by overlaying the two truth boundaries diagrams in Figure 16, bringing awareness to areas of

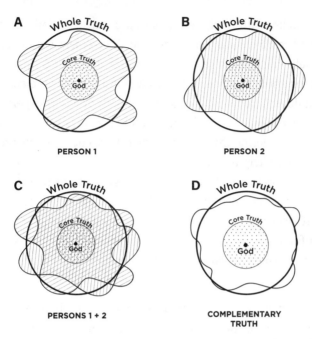

Figure 16. Visualization of the truth boundaries diagrams (A and B) of two different people. We can either reject the different beliefs of someone with a different truth boundaries diagram than us, or we can love and seek to understand them, without compromising our core truth. In this way, we overlap the diagrams and gain access to further truth, confirmation, awareness, and understanding. Truth boundaries diagram for **A** person 1 and **B** person 2. **C:** Overlapping the two diagrams creates a thatched region showing shared truths and distinctly marked regions representing distinctly held truths of persons 1 and 2. **D:** What is possible when collectively seeking complementary truths and expanding/refining closer to the whole truth—this is a combination of the truths from person 1 and person 2, with the boundaries that extended far outside the whole truth pulled in through learning and edification.

agreement and indicating potential space for understanding new truth. Doing so doesn't have to compromise the core truths of the gospel for which you are uncompromising. President Dieter F. Uchtdorf provided timely warnings and counsel on this topic:

> Part of the reason for poor judgment comes from the tendency of mankind to blur the line between belief and truth. We too often

confuse belief with truth, thinking that because something makes sense or is convenient, it must be true. Conversely, we sometimes don't believe truth or reject it—because it would require us to change or admit that we were wrong. Often, truth is rejected because it doesn't appear to be consistent with previous experiences.

When the opinions or "truths" of others contradict our own, instead of considering the possibility that there could be information that might be helpful and augment or complement what we know, we often jump to conclusions or make assumptions that the other person is misinformed, mentally challenged, or even intentionally trying to deceive.

Unfortunately, this tendency can spread to all areas of our lives—from sports to family relationships and from religion to politics.[3]

There are certainly falsehoods to what may be hawked as truth in our world; we can be alert to these while also being mindful not to fall victim to the fallacy of wholly rejecting any new way of thinking presented to us. This takes work, but it is a work worth doing in all categories of truth seeking in our lives.

Applying the Principles

1. **Prioritize love of God and others:** Always remember that the most essential elements supporting our spiritual journey are loving God and loving others—these are pillars and core truths. As you navigate through life, ensure that these pillars remain strong, as they are the foundation that will carry you to lasting peace and joy. Regularly assess where your attention and efforts are directed. Are you more concerned with the decorative elements of your spiritual journey— the achievements, knowledge, recognition, and accomplishments— or with strengthening the core principles that truly support your

progress on the covenant path of becoming like Christ? Keep the pillars strong by focusing on what matters most.

2. **Avoid judging a whole person based on one part:** Just as I was unable to notice the difference between a raw egg and a hard-boiled egg based only on how they looked and felt, it's also naïve to believe you can accurately judge everything about a person based on only a few pieces of information. Seek to truly understand individuals and to love as the Savior loves. If His ministry taught us anything, it is that He sees past the labels we give ourselves and others and seeks out "the one."

3. **Be a peacemaker:** In a world filled with contention and division, strive to be a source of peace. True disciples build, lift, and inspire others regardless of the situation. Make a conscious effort to find common ground and strengthen the bonds of love and understanding with those around you, *especially* those with differing views.

4. **Engage in self-reflection:** Just as the master craftsman in the parable felt the tremor in the bridge and examined the pillars, regularly reflect on your own spiritual foundations. Are there cracks forming due to neglect, misprioritization, or pride? Take time to repair and reinforce your commitment to the core truths of the gospel. Trust in the guidance of the prophets, who, like the master craftsman, provide warnings and counsel to help you maintain a strong foundation.

5. **Be patient and open to complementary truths:** When you find someone has different beliefs than you, seek to understand their perspective, learn about their background and circumstances—doing so with patience and openness can either expand your truth boundaries to encompass new truths, pull in boundaries that are extending beyond the whole truth, or increase confidence in the current boundaries you have set. No matter what, you will be better for showing compassion and having real interest.

In a world where distractions and falsehoods abound, it is essential to maintain a clear focus on what truly matters. The parable of the bridge serves as a reminder that the core truths of the gospel of Jesus Christ, including loving God and others, are what sustain us, even when everything else might seem in disarray. As you move forward in your spiritual journey, you should prioritize these foundational truths, engage in self-reflection, and seek to build peace and understanding with others. By doing so, you will ensure that the pillars of your faith remain strong, enabling you to have ongoing access to lasting peace and joy.

Chapter 6

"LO, HERE" AND "LO, THERE": DISCERNING TRUTH AMID THE NOISE

We had to learn how to react to things we never would have expected or imagined. That's what the training was for. And sure enough, when we got there, the unexpected happened.

—Neil Armstrong

What would you consider the most stressful, scary, or nerve-racking minutes of your life? Perhaps it was a big event where you had to speak, or a major exam you dreaded, meeting someone you'd long anticipated, or a time when you or a loved one was sick or injured. For Neil Armstrong and Buzz Aldrin, the answer is clear: some of the most harrowing minutes of their lives were undoubtedly the thirteen minutes they spent descending to the lunar surface during the Apollo 11 mission—the first moon landing.

From the moment their Lunar Module (LM) detached from the Command Module (CM) as they orbited the moon, Armstrong and Aldrin were embarking on countless "firsts." It was the first time humans had descended to the lunar surface, the first time the LM's computer—an entirely custom and new technology—was used to assist with an actual landing, the first time NASA communicated with the LM as it maneuvered its way down to the Sea of Tranquility 240,000 miles from Earth, the first time a craft of this size and weight had attempted to land safely on the surface, and much more.

The achievements of the Apollo program have become even more impressive in recent years as modern technology continues to struggle with successful moon landings. One example is the lunar lander Odysseus, developed by US-based company Intuitive Machines. Despite the latest technology in communications, controls, and sensors, the unmanned craft tipped onto its side during its landing in February of 2024, rendering it unable to generate enough solar power to stay in communication or to complete its mission.[*] Just one month earlier, the Japanese space agency faced a similar setback when its SLIM (Smart Lander for Investigating Moon) spacecraft experienced an engine failure during descent, resulting in a misaligned landing that left SLIM essentially upside down.[†] Some have suggested that, in contrast to these recent mishaps by high-tech robots, the success of the Apollo moon landings was due in part to the presence of humans, who could make real-time judgment calls and adapt to unforeseen circumstances—capabilities that computer-controlled systems have yet to match.[‡]

I hope this highlights just how incredible it was that the Apollo 11 mission achieved a successful landing on the moon and return to Earth

---

[*] For coverage on this, see: Marcia Dunn, "Sideways moon landing cuts mission short, private US lunar lander will stop working Tuesday," *AP News*, 26 February 2024; available at https://apnews.com/article/moon-landing-private-nasa-28fdcd5ce5b50586d 3feee68ae26864c; accessed 31 October 2024. Pictures from a press conference showing a small model of Odysseus on its side are really striking—so much work and technology that made it so far, only to trip and break a leg during landing and fall over.

[†] For coverage on this, see: Andrew Jones, "Japan's SLIM moon lander stages unexpected revival after lunar night," *Space News*, 26 February 2024; available at https://spacenews .com/japans-slim-moon-lander-stages-unexpected-revival-after-lunar-night/; accessed 31 October 2024. In this case, a small lunar rover (the LEV-2) captured an actual picture of the upside-down spacecraft on the lunar surface.

[‡] See, for example: Sharmila Kuthunur, "'Everything has changed since Apollo': Why landing on the moon is still incredibly difficult in 2024," *Live Science*, 1 March 2024; available at https://www.livescience.com/space/the-moon/everything-has-changed -since-apollo-why-landing-on-the-moon-is-still-incredibly-difficult-in-2024; accessed 31 October 2024.

back in 1969! The NASA team, including the astronauts, had trained for thousands of hours leading up to the final thirteen minutes of approach to the moon. For weeks, they ran the lunar landing scenario dozens of times, with new challenges thrown at them each time. After each simulation, they'd debrief, then run another. One of the NASA flight controllers (in the Houston mission control center) said, "If you can survive the simulations, the mission is a piece of cake."[1] Yet, despite all the prep, they still encountered challenges that were not expected, as Armstrong said in the quote that begins this chapter. So how did they get through them?

It turns out there are some compelling parallels between how the astronauts of Apollo 11 managed to successfully complete their lunar landing and our efforts to navigate the onslaught of fact and fiction surrounding us today. The astronauts needed information—either through training or active communication—for making fast decisions. *We* need truth, either known or newly received, for cutting through the falsehoods and pressing forward on the covenant path in all aspects of our life. In short, we need to discern truth amid the noise of the world. There are four principles of the Apollo 11 success that we will relate to how we can discern truth: preparation, knowing the communicators, alignment, and focus.

Preparation

While there were some unexpected challenges during the Apollo 11 moon landing, many obstacles had already been encountered during countless simulations. In one of their final training exercises simulating the lunar landing, the simulation team triggered a "1202" error code on the computer. This alarm caught the entire team of engineers in mission control off guard, leading them to scramble for a solution. Due to delays in decision-making, the simulated landing was ultimately aborted. As it turned out, the 1202 alarm—one of hundreds of potential error codes— was not grounds for an abort. It simply indicated that the computer was heavily loaded with tasks and would have to prioritize them, serving more as a warning light than a critical failure.

After that simulation, one of the engineers made a reference sheet of all similar computer alarms and how to quickly react to them (there were so many that they could not possibly simulate them all). Then, just a few weeks later, as Armstrong and Aldrin were descending toward the lunar surface in the LM, an alarm suddenly blared and flashed. Armstrong, with uncharacteristic urgency in his voice, is heard saying, "Give us a reading on the 1202 Program Alarm."[2] With the astronauts' heart rates spiking as reactionary impulses kicked in under the stressful sound of the blaring alarms, 240,000 miles away, an engineer was able to quickly shuffle through the prepared papers at his workstation and respond, "We're a go on that alarm"—meaning, it's ok, we can proceed!

The stress and fear and uncertainty of certain circumstances can cause anyone to lose their footing without some stabilizing support. Just as the astronauts needed helpful information as quickly as possible when alarms were sounding, we also need truth that instructs and supports us through our questions and trials. Instead of going to the moon and back, our mission in mortality is articulated by the apostle Paul to the Ephesians:

> Till we all come in the unity of the faith, and of the knowledge of the Son of God, unto a perfect man, unto the measure of the stature of the fulness of Christ. (Ephesians 4:13)

With that goal in mind, Paul then points out the considerable challenges to this mission:

> That we henceforth be no more children, tossed to and fro, and carried about with every wind of doctrine, by the sleight of men, and cunning craftiness, whereby they lie in wait to deceive. (Ephesians 4:14)

Our world today presents an increasing array of alarms—some real and important to address, others false and merely distractions. These alarms can take the form of opposition that tosses our faith "to and fro" (Ephesians 4:14) if it is not deeply rooted within us. We are surrounded by shouts of "Lo, here!" and "lo, there!" (Luke 17:21; see also Joseph Smith—History 1:5) that may distract or deceive us. Some of these shouts may come from well-intentioned people, but the substance they offer is often tainted with falsehoods they have mistakenly embraced as facts. Pressing forward in this dizzying landscape requires more than just determination—it demands preparation.

Preparation against the flood of facts and fictions in the world means securing ourselves to the anchor of truth: our Savior, Jesus Christ, who is "the way, the truth, and the life" (John 14:6). Jesus made this proclamation after telling His disciples that He would prepare a place for them and "receive [them] unto [Himself]" and that "whither [He goes] ye know, and the way ye know" (John 14:2–4). Upon hearing this, Thomas asked, "Lord, we know not whither thou goest; and how can we know the way?" (John 14:5).

Thomas's confusion seems understandable, given the details we have of this conversation. The disciples often took Jesus's words literally and expected immediate or near-term fulfillment. So when Jesus told them He was preparing a place for them and that they knew the way, they might have thought He meant they would meet up with Him soon, perhaps within days or weeks. Thomas realized Jesus was speaking of something deeper—a truth yet to be revealed—only to discover that the truth was Jesus Himself.

So, what *does* it mean that Jesus is the way? Looking back to the verses from Ephesians we quoted above, it is our "knowledge of the Son of God" and our stature growing into the "fulness of Christ" (Ephesians 4:13) that will protect us from being "carried about with every wind of doctrine, by the sleight of men, and cunning craftiness, whereby they lie in wait to deceive" (Ephesians 4:14). In short, as we study, believe, and live the word of God, it will prepare us against the storms of information and distraction that lie ahead.

When the storms do arrive, we must remember that we can only reliably draw from what we have obtained. If we seek to teach others by the power of God, we must "first seek to obtain [the word of God]" (Doctrine and Covenants 11:21). If we want protection from temptation and falsehoods or the "fiery darts of the adversary" that seek to blind us and lead us to destruction, we must "give heed unto the word of the Lord" by holding "fast unto it" (1 Nephi 15:24–25). When we are frequently reminded to study the scriptures and to be prepared to hear God daily, it is about preparation and fortification—obtaining and heeding the word of God.

Just as the Apollo 11 mission was saved from a likely abort thanks to the preparation of seemingly endless simulations, our mission to the place our Savior has prepared will rely on our preparations for success. We don't only study the gospel for inspiration that may come in the moment, but for preparation against the moments ahead, when our perseverance will depend on our hold to the word of God to keep us in the path of truth.

Know the Communicators

One of my favorite podcast series of all time is the BBC-produced program called *13 Minutes to the Moon*. In Season 1, the host presents the story of the people behind the Apollo 11 lunar landing. Highlights and interviews are given with the various voices from NASA's mission control in Houston, providing insight into the communication that was happening throughout those stressful minutes.

If you were to listen to the full thirteen minutes of audio taking place on the mission control channel without some training or preparation, you'd hear too many people talking all at once, static, technical lingo, and the occasional recognizable word. Each episode of the podcast breaks down a stretch of the audio—interviewing the people involved, what they're saying, and what sort of preparation had gone into that moment. The final episode of the season is the raw thirteen minutes of audio, which you can then listen to with new ears, picking out some of those nail-biting moments and the people behind the voices you hear responding. It's amazing!

This is one example of the power of knowing the communicators for improving how you find truth in the world. But there's one more relevant aspect from the Apollo missions: It would be too distracting for the astronauts in the spacecraft to have to listen to all the chatter on the mission control line, so there is one person, the "CapCom," designated to listen to the channel and then communicate the relevant information to the spacecraft. The CapCom was always a fellow astronaut. The astronauts had trained as a group and knew each other well while also being equally familiar with the mission needs and processes. This, combined with their shared understanding of spaceflight, allowed the CapCom to be a familiar voice who could ensure clear and effective communication to the astronauts during the critical moments of a mission.

These examples demonstrate the importance of knowing the communicators from whom you're seeking to understand truth. The better we know someone, the easier they are to understand amid other distractions we may be experiencing. "Learn of me, and listen to my words" (Doctrine and Covenants 19:23), the Lord invites, promising peace and comprehension of truth in return (see Doctrine and Covenants 88:67). The Savior also declares that life eternal itself is to know "the only true God, and Jesus Christ, whom [God] hast sent" (John 17:3). Interesting that He points out the *only true* God, acknowledging there are many other "gods" that people often come to know far better than their Heavenly Father.

One of the most compelling titles and concepts of the Savior is that of Good Shepherd. There is a beautiful painting by the artist Yongsung Kim titled *One Fold and One Shepherd* that depicts Jesus as a shepherd among a flock of sheep. Most of the sheep are grazing, not seeming to pay much attention to Him, though they are close by. A few are looking at Jesus as if awaiting His command. Some of the sheep are far from Him, including one who looks to be wandering away and is noticeably less illuminated than the others. Meanwhile, Jesus is earnestly looking out into the field as if searching for any who have strayed from His flock. With this image in mind, consider the Savior's teachings:

> And when he putteth forth his own sheep, he goeth before them, and the sheep follow him: *for they know his voice.*
>
> And a stranger will they not follow, but will flee from him: for they know not the voice of strangers. . . .
>
> I am the good shepherd, and know my sheep, *and am known of mine.* (John 10:4–5, 14; emphasis added)

As we come to know more about Christ, our ability to see and recognize truth, which is light (see Doctrine and Covenants 88:6–7), increases. And we don't have to worry about whether He will be speaking since He *always is*—He is the "shepherd [who] hath called after you and is still calling after you" (Alma 5:37). Just as the astronauts trusted in communication with other astronauts and how familiarity with the people and voices of mission control made it possible to pick out important information from noise, so can we find truth in this world as we come to familiarize ourselves with the Savior and the voice of His Spirit.

Alignment

One of the most frustrating and unexpected issues during the first moon landing was the difficulty mission control had in establishing a stable communication signal with the astronauts. For the first seven to eight minutes of lunar descent, there were repeated communication failures. The astronauts were hurtling toward the moon in the LM, embarking on countless "firsts" and needing help to monitor the many signals coming into the spacecraft, yet all they heard from Earth was static—and vice versa. This communication breakdown was the first issue that nearly led to an abort, because if mission control couldn't receive data from the LM, then the astronauts would be flying unsupported, with only a first-of-its-kind computer to aid them.

During those unsettling minutes, mission control relayed instructions to the third astronaut, Mike Collins, who was still in the CM, orbiting the moon. He in turn passed those instructions on to Armstrong and Aldrin in the LM. The guidance from mission control was to reposition the LM so the antenna would have a more direct path for communication with Earth. It took a few tries, but they eventually managed to roll the craft enough to restore the signal. Some key decision points were passed during that interval of signal loss, forcing the team to make judgment calls on whether to proceed ("go!") or abort. This was yet another instance where a computer might have aborted the mission since they'd passed critical milestones, but humans could judge the situation based on the data they had last received and their instinct for what was happening.

Alignment between the LM antenna and receiving satellites on Earth enabled clearer communication, just as our alignment with heaven improves our communication with God:

> If any man will do his will, he shall know of the doctrine, whether it be of God, or whether I speak of myself. (John 7:17)

This point is rather obvious—obedience brings alignment and more clarity in our connection with heaven. Let's focus on another aspect from the Apollo 11 analogy: How do we react when we're misaligned? In spiritual communications, misalignment can be caused by disobedience, thus the importance of daily repentance.* But whether misalignment is caused by disobedience or if we just happen to find ourselves in a situation where the heavens are quiet at a time when we feel we need God most—how do we react in these moments of greatest need?

In the case of Apollo 11, the astronauts and mission control remained focused on the mission they'd all set out to accomplish. The loss of expected data was frustrating and gnawed at their confidence that all was well, but they relied on the most recent data they'd received and pressed forward with it. They could have tossed their manuals in the air, bashed the control panel, and smashed the abort button. After all, wasn't communication supposed to be part of this mission? Weren't they supposed to have a constant connection (a "companion" if you will)? But that's not what they did; they didn't allow the frustration of the moment to compromise all they'd worked for in the years leading up to those moments.

Do we let the environment or heat of the moment rob us of years of effort? Just because we may not be receiving things in the timing or manner we'd planned doesn't mean the Lord isn't calling out and guiding us in ways we cannot see. There is power in holding on to the truth we have and pressing forward through the occasional mists or static, not allowing them to loosen our grip on the word of God. As Elder Dieter F. Uchtdorf taught:

> When you earnestly seek the truth—eternal, unchanging truth—your choices become much clearer. Yes, you still have temptation and trials. Bad things still happen. Puzzling things.

---

* As President Russell M. Nelson counseled: "Nothing is more liberating, more ennobling, or more crucial to our individual progression than is a regular, daily focus on repentance. Repentance is not an event; it is a process. It is the key to happiness and peace of mind. When coupled with faith, repentance opens our access to the power of the Atonement of Jesus Christ." Russell M. Nelson, "We Can Do Better and Be Better," *Ensign*, May 2019.

Tragic things. But you can manage when you know who you are, why you are here, and when you trust God.[3]

There is a hierarchy to truth when it comes to its impact on our calm and peace in the midst of turmoil. Holding on to the eternal truths of the gospel of Jesus Christ can provide a peace that "passeth all understanding" (Philippians 4:7).

Focus

Staying focused in NASA's mission control room was essential. Each person there had a specific job monitoring something important for the mission, from astronaut vital signs to spacecraft fuel level. If something were to suddenly go wrong—which could happen at any point—they needed to make sure a message could come through. Considering there was a four-second delay in receiving communications from the astronauts in lunar orbit, a crisp and well-controlled protocol for focus within mission control was imperative.

This is one aspect that Hollywood often gets wrong. If you've seen depictions of mission control, like in the 1995 film *Apollo 13*, you've probably seen engineers cheering and high-fiving when something goes well. First of all, engineers don't celebrate like football players—we're nerds, remember? Second, making any noise or commotion in mission control would be a serious violation! Even after the successful landing on the Moon was confirmed, there was no time for hugs—they had further checks to run to decide whether to stay or leave immediately.

Staying focused on the gospel of Jesus Christ means a determination to not compromise your faith in the midst of pressure. That's not to say you can't celebrate victories or bemoan struggles—but that you don't allow circumstances to manipulate your dependence on God and submission to Him. Consistent with the previous point, you stay aligned.

One of my favorite examples of the power of focusing on the Lord comes from Lehi's vision in 1 Nephi 8. The landscape of the vision is spelled out in Lehi's description of the tree, straight and narrow path, rod of iron along the path, field, mists of darkness, river of water, and great and spacious building. Just think of all the possibilities for distraction in this environment! After Nephi believed and prepared himself, he received the same vision and was able to answer many questions from his brothers about what various things meant. Some of Nephi's understanding came after he asked questions of his own to the Spirit of the Lord (see 1 Nephi 11).

In Lehi's description of the vision, he indicated there was "a river of water; and it ran along, and it was near the tree of which I was partaking the fruit" (1 Nephi 8:13). The rod of iron, which led to the tree, "extended along the bank of the river" (1 Nephi 8:19). "On the other side of the river of water" there stood a "great and spacious building" (1 Nephi 8:26). So, this river is a notable part of the landscape, but not given much description in terms of its meaning. Hence, the following interchange between Nephi and his brothers:

> And they said unto me: What meaneth the river of water which our father saw?
>
> And I said unto them that the water which my father saw was filthiness; and so much was his mind swallowed up in other things that he beheld not the filthiness of the water. (1 Nephi 15:26–27)

Lehi was so focused on the tree and on finding his family and bringing them together that he did not even notice the filthiness of the river's water. He was aware of the river's presence, acknowledging its place in the landscape (he wasn't going to inadvertently fall in), but he remained unaffected by its filthiness because his mind was fully engaged in other matters—things that aligned with his ultimate goals.

When it comes to identifying truth, having the focus that Lehi demonstrated can make greater things known to us. The Lord promises that if we "sanctify [ourselves] that [our] minds become single to God" then we will "see him; for he will unveil his face unto [us]" (Doctrine and Covenants 88:68). We have an example of such singularity in focus leading to an opening of the veil and a vision of the Son of God: the brother of Jared. After appearing to the brother of Jared, the Savior explains, "never has man believed in me as thou hast" (Ether 3:15).

By remaining focused on our ultimate goal of coming to a "knowledge of the Son of God, unto a perfect man, unto the measure of the stature of the fulness of Christ" (Ephesians 4:13), we will be ready to receive incredible truths; just as the brother of Jared, who was shown "all the inhabitants of the earth which had been, and also all that would be . . . even unto the ends of the earth" (Ether 3:25).

Distraction Versus Traction

It's fun to connect aspects of the Apollo 11 moon landing with how we find truth amid the incessant noise of information in our daily lives. However, despite the strong parallels that can be drawn, I recognize many of the takeaways are generally motivating but not necessarily directly applicable. For instance, it's helpful to know that we should have our minds focused on the Lord and be aligned with Him through obedience and daily repentance, but how does that translate to dealing with neverending social media posts/reels, pressure from friends, or strong messages inconsistent with our core beliefs?

We need to have strategies in place that can help us convert our internal and external triggers into actions that bring us more truth and light. There are principles for dealing with distractions, particularly those coming from technology, taught by author and entrepreneur Nir Eyal.*

---

* See Nir's book for insights: Nir Eyal, *Indistractable: How to Control Your Attention and Choose Your Life* (Dallas, TX: BenBella Books, 2019). There are also many articles that discuss his strategies on his website: www.nirandfar.com. The strategies summarized here are from one of those articles.

His perspective is that there aren't any good antonyms for the word *distraction*, so he poses the word *traction* as an appropriate option (it certainly makes sense from a word construction point of view!).[4] Nir identifies *distraction* as "actions that move us away from what we really want" and *traction* as "actions that move us toward what we really want." Anything that's happening to us, whether externally or internally, is a trigger that translates either to distraction or traction. You can see this illustrated in Figure 17.

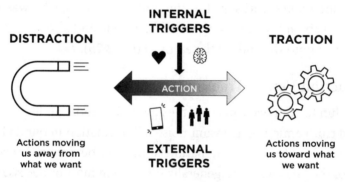

Figure 17. Diagram showing how our actions are a result of internal or external triggers. The actions we take either move us away from what we want (distraction) or toward what we want (traction). Employing strategies for being "indistractable" helps with the goal of finding and retaining the truth of all things.

There are four strategies to becoming "indistractable" according to Nir, and I believe these map well to our goal of finding more truth amid the noise and mass information of the world. The steps are:

1. *Master internal triggers.* Most of the time we choose distraction to mask bad feelings. For instance, we may doubt our self-worth, think any level of effort will not make a difference, or be overwhelmed by the monotony of certain tasks. Identifying the feeling or thought that caused us distraction,

writing it down and keeping a log, allows us to then practice turning those triggers into traction.

2. *Make time for traction.* This is part of controlling the external triggers—create them yourself! Set a block of time in your schedule for doing things that bring traction, such as daily scripture study, time with family, going to the temple, providing service, and so forth. For most people, if they're not intentional in this way, these things will rarely happen.

3. *Hack back external triggers.* Nir poses a compelling question: Is an "external trigger serving you, or are you serving it?"[5] If something leads to distraction, it should be eliminated. Think about notifications on your phone and what they lead you to do. If it's to take time to call a loved one to check on them—great! If it's to give your attention to an app that doesn't help you achieve what you want—not great.

4. *Prevent distraction with pacts.* This one has excellent gospel symmetry. We make covenants with God as a pact to strive to follow and become like Him. We can also create pacts with family members or friends that apply a form of accountability to our efforts to becoming indistractable. It's good to have a reminder of the covenants we have made with God, hence the power of attending the temple.

If you're anything like me, then you already had a few things come to your mind that could help in your life. Any effort to convert more of our triggers into traction that brings us to our goal will be worth it! It doesn't matter whether we are a team of thousands with a goal of putting humans on the moon and bringing them back again, or an individual with a goal of being Christlike and receiving more truth; there are triggers with the ability to distract us or give us traction to reach our goal.

Applying the Principles

1. **Develop discernment:** In a world filled with conflicting voices, cultivate the ability to discern truth through increased spiritual sensitivity. Consider ways that you could increase the presence of the gospel basics in your daily life: prayer, scripture study, pondering, and so forth. The more familiar you are with the Lord's "voice," the better you will be able to pick it out from amid the noise.

2. **Focus on core gospel truths:** Anchor yourself in the foundational truths of the gospel, which will help you navigate through the noise and distractions of the world. When confronted with information that does not align with these truths, do not compromise or discard what you already know is true to accommodate new, uncertain ideas. Explore them with openness that does not include loosening your hold on the word of God.

3. **Trust in your preparation:** Rely on the years of preparation you have undoubtedly put into obtaining the truths you hold. The Holy Ghost will help you discern between truth and error. His influence is vital in cutting through the confusion and finding clarity, especially when faced with complex or challenging situations.

4. **Have patience with the Lord:** There will be times of frustrating signal loss, where it will be our duty to "wait on the Lord: be of good courage, and he shall strengthen thine heart: wait, I say, on the Lord" (Psalm 27:14). Trust in the eternal truths you have already received and the confidence that God is there, even if you don't recognize His guidance at present.

5. **Increase your traction:** As outlined in the previous section, implement strategies to turn distractions into actions that bring you closer to your goals. Start with something small, like intentionally carving out a few minutes each day for an activity that enhances

your spiritual or personal growth. Over time, these small actions will build momentum, helping you stay focused on what truly matters.

The world will not relent in bombarding us with distractions, noise, and an overwhelming amount of information. As the analogy of the Apollo 11 moon landing exemplifies, maintaining focus on our mission, aligning ourselves with the source of truth, knowing the communicator, and being prepared will enable us to access the truth we seek amid the turmoil. There are practical ways to combat the noise, and even small, intentional steps can make a noticeable difference. Above all, we need to increase our familiarity with the Lord's voice, in whatever manner He is communicating with us.

Chapter 7

COMMUNICATING WITH GOD, THE SOURCE OF ALL TRUTH

We are all in the gutter, but some of us are looking at the stars.

—Oscar Wilde

Years ago, I took my twelve-year-old daughter with me on a work trip to France. We spent a day traveling outside of Paris to visit the famously opulent Palace of Versailles. Our tour package included a guided tour with a guide who shared insightful stories and details as we walked through the palace and its grounds. Due to the cacophony of clamoring crowds at nearly every step, the guide provided each member of our small group with a radio headset. He spoke into a microphone that broadcast his voice directly to our headsets and it worked remarkably well!

At one point during the tour, I slipped my headset off and glanced around at the noisy crowd. I realized that even though the other tourists were walking through the same space as our small group, they were having a vastly different experience. While we stopped at specific points to focus on a painting or display, captivated by our guide's stories, most people merely glanced and walked by, comparatively indifferent. Although surrounded by the same scenery, their understanding was limited, drowned out by the din of the multitude, in stark contrast to the engaging narratives we were enjoying.

In like manner, our experience in mortality can be vastly different from that of others even when sharing the same physical space. There is a "light which shineth, which giveth [us] light, . . . which is the same light that quickeneth [our] understandings" (Doctrine and Covenants 88:11) and this "light proceedeth forth from the presence of God to fill the immensity of space" (88:12); yet, despite this universal presence of literal enlightenment, for many "the light shineth in darkness, and the darkness comprehendeth it not" (88:49).

Communication with Light

When we speak of light scientifically, it's referred to as electromagnetic radiation, which comes in a broad range of different energies or wavelengths (think different colors of visible light). Of the countless uses of light harnessed by humans, from enabling sight to generating images of the body's organs with medical scans, perhaps the most incredible is its use in communication. Attributes of light are modified to encode data into photons ("pieces" of light), which are transmitted across the earth at speeds faster than any other known energy source. With the appropriate receiver device, the data that is packed into the light can then be decoded and accessed.

Think about the last time you retrieved information from an electronic device. Was it a video call answered on your smartphone? Perhaps a radio station you tuned in to in your car? Maybe a social media page that you reloaded? In each of these instances you used a receiver that was decoding information transmitted to it using light. And what would have happened to that information if you hadn't picked it up with your receiver and focused your attention on it—would it still have existed? Absolutely—just as the tour guide's voice was still transmitted via radio waves during my visit to Versailles, regardless of whether I or the rest of our group had our headsets activated to listen.

Light and Truth

The scriptures present a synonymous connection between light and truth:

> For the word of the Lord is truth, and whatsoever is truth is light, and whatsoever is light is Spirit, even the Spirit of Jesus Christ. (Doctrine and Covenants 84:45)
>
> He comprehended all things, that he might be in all and through all things; the light of truth; which truth shineth. This is the light of Christ. (Doctrine and Covenants 88:6–7)

To improve our understanding of this light and truth connection, let's consider what we know. Scientifically, we know that light moves faster than anything else and can be used for carrying vast amounts of information—nearly all data that's transmitted in our modern age is done so using light. Doctrinally, we know that light fills the immensity of space and has an integral connection to truth, wherein receiving one brings with it the other. A simple merge of these two principles related to light suggests that truth may be encoded into *spiritual* light that's accessible to those who are sufficiently tuned in to receive it:

> He that keepeth his commandments receiveth truth and light, until he is glorified in truth and knoweth all things. (Doctrine and Covenants 93:28)

By embracing and living truth, we gain access to more and more truth, carried on energetic waves of heavenly light; this is akin to how increasing the brightness or intensity of visible light improves our discernment or visibility of what is around us:

> That which is of God is light; and he that receiveth light, and continueth in God, receiveth more light; and that light groweth brighter and brighter until the perfect day. (Doctrine and Covenants 50:24)

Thinking about the truths of eternity being carried on waves of spiritual light that fill the immensity of space and are available to anyone may be a new way of considering this truth-and-light connection. Yet being surrounded by information-packed light that you are completely unaware of is part of each moment of our lives. Right now, wherever you are reading this book, you are swarmed by light waves carrying local and satellite radio stations, television channels, and cellular and Wi-Fi data. Just because you're not accessing all the information from this multitude of light waves doesn't mean it isn't there and available.

The same may be true with spiritual light.* Truth-carrying waves of light are always available, but access to the truth is gated by certain principles. Elder Bruce R. McConkie taught this concept as he reflected on a time when he visited a TV station broadcasting center and connected what he learned there to spiritual light and revealed truth:

> Now I think this illustrates perfectly what is involved in the receipt of revelation and the seeing of visions. We can read about visions and revelations in the records of the past, . . . but we cannot comprehend what is involved until we see and hear and experience for ourselves. . . .
>
> And so it is with the revelations and visions of eternity. They are around us all the time. . . .
>
> But millions of people everywhere live and die without tasting the good word of God, because they do not obey the laws which implant the revelations of the Lord in their souls.[1]

This perspective on the revelations of eternity absolutely fascinates me. It says so much about God's desire for us to receive all that He has.

---

* Further discussion around possible connections between the physical properties of light and how it functions spiritually can be found in my previous book: Aaron D. Franklin, *The Spiritual Physics of Light: How We See, Feel, and Know Truth* (Provo, UT, and Salt Lake City: BYU Religious Studies Center and Deseret Book, 2021).

It also explains how there are eternal truths available and accessed by people from all cultures, religions, and places across the globe.

"Hear Him"

This view of how heavenly truth and guidance is always around us was transformative for me a few years ago. In commemoration of the 200th anniversary of the First Vision, President Russell M. Nelson reminded us of the importance of increasing our capacity to receive personal revelation. He taught:

> Our Father knows that when we are surrounded by uncertainty and fear, what will help us the very most is to hear His Son.
>
> Because when we seek to hear—truly hear—His Son, we will be guided to know what to do in any circumstance. . . .
>
> In those two words—"Hear Him"—God gives us the pattern for success, happiness, and joy in this life. . . .
>
> As we seek to be disciples of Jesus Christ, our efforts to *hear Him* need to be ever more intentional. It takes conscious and consistent effort to fill our daily lives with His words, His teachings, His truths.[2]

Following this inspiring instruction, the Church launched the "Hear Him" campaign, which has included dozens of Church leaders providing examples of how they "personally 'hear' the Lord Jesus Christ through the Spirit."*

I spent months earnestly trying to follow President Nelson's counsel, but despite my efforts, it seemed the Lord was not speaking to me any more than before.

I redoubled my efforts. I refined the questions I was asking in my

* This quote, along with a collection of the videos related to "Hear Him," are available on the Church's website here: https://www.churchofjesuschrist.org/media/collection/hear -him?lang=eng; accessed 4 November 2024.

personal prayers, amplifying my focus on repentance, and sought more opportunities to serve others. All of these were (and are) spiritually rewarding, but none seemed to thin the barrier that felt present between my supplications and heaven's response.

Around this time, I'd been working on revisions for my book *The Spiritual Physics of Light*, in which I explore some of the possible connections between the physical properties of light and its spiritual attributes—just as we discussed briefly in the previous sections of this chapter. It was then that it occurred to me: I've been trying to get God to speak to me more, when in reality He already *has* spoken, *is* speaking, and will *continue* to speak—it's just a matter of me tuning in! I'd been thinking of my communication with God like a telephone and was waiting impatiently for God to call or to answer. Instead, it's more like a radio, where He's already spoken and it's just up to me to tune in and trust that the message is being received (even when it can be difficult to tell).

This was a landmark realization for me. I know the difference may seem subtle—that I'm not trying to get God to speak but rather trying to hear Him—but it allowed me to recognize that because He's always speaking, I can trust that He's there whenever I strive to listen. I realized that the barriers I felt between the heavens and my prayers were of my own making, mostly related to how I expected the Spirit to communicate with me. By removing those barriers, I also expanded my confidence that the Spirit may often speak in ways I don't immediately recognize. Yet as I press forward on the covenant path, I can trust I am being led to greater and greater truth.

When we were discussing this change in perspective about how God communicates to us, my wife, Lianne, had a powerful way of framing things. She said whenever she's wondering about God speaking to her regarding a certain topic or question she's praying about, instead of wondering "is He?" she reassures herself that "He is." The simple rearrangement of two short words transforms uncertainty to confidence.

This confidence is born out of earnestly and faithfully seeking truth from God, and it means we don't have to require bold manifestations that are seen or heard in order to trust that the Spirit is guiding us.

Blindness of Mind

It can be helpful to reflect on situations where truth was available to us from the Spirit, but we failed to access it. There may be no better example of this than the contrast between the faithful Nephi and his brothers Laman and Lemuel. While Nephi put forth the effort to achieve a singleness of focus on the Lord and thus received great truths, Laman and Lemuel complained, "the Lord maketh no such thing known unto us" (1 Nephi 15:9). To which Nephi replied:

> Do ye not remember the things which the Lord hath said?—
> If ye will not harden your hearts, and ask me in faith, believing that ye shall receive, with diligence in keeping my commandments, surely these things shall be made known unto you. (1 Nephi 15:11)

Hardness of heart is one possibility for not receiving truth from the Spirit. Another phrase often connected to having a hardness of heart is "blindness of mind" (see 3 Nephi 7:16 or 1 Nephi 7:8) and, interestingly, they almost always appear together. After all, the Lord has been clear in His requirement of both "the heart and a willing mind" (Doctrine and Covenants 64:34), which are also part of the list of requirements for faithfully serving the Lord: heart, might, mind, and strength (see Doctrine and Covenants 4:2; 59:5; 98:47).

Can you think of a time when you had a blindness of mind? For me, these are the instances when my own evaluation of circumstances and probabilities got in the way of my willingness to trust in God. These are when the "learned think they are wise, and they hearken not unto the counsel of God . . . supposing they know of themselves" (2 Nephi 9:28).

Such blindness of mind invariably leads to a hardness of heart, taking our soul out of tune with the reception of truth and keeping us in darkness.

Another aspect of having blindness of mind when seeking for gospel truth is "looking beyond the mark" (mentioned as a cause of blindness of mind in Jacob 4:14). Elder Quentin L. Cook taught the following about this:

> Today there is a tendency among some of us to "look beyond the mark" rather than to maintain a testimony of gospel basics. We do this when we substitute the philosophies of men for gospel truths, engage in gospel extremism, seek heroic gestures at the expense of daily consecration, or elevate rules over doctrine. Avoiding these behaviors will help us avoid the theological blindness and stumbling that Jacob described. . . .
>
> When we look beyond the mark, we are looking beyond Christ, the only name under heaven whereby we might be saved.[3]

The impact of blindness of mind is not just manifest in seeking for gospel truth. This phrase may be the scriptural language but being intentionally blind to ideas or conclusions that push against those we've held for a long time is stunting to our search for truth holistically. Blindness of mind more simply put is pride. It's possible to keep hold of truth we've validated, particularly core gospel truth, while open-mindedly learning about other perspectives, experiences, and beliefs. The most troubling manifestation of blindness of mind is when a person is so doggedly fixated on their own narrative that they vilify anyone who sees differently by labeling them deceived, or other name-calling and belittling dismissiveness. No difference in perspective on a topic is more important than how we treat those with the differing perspective (as always, the supreme example is the Lord, Jesus Christ). Trying to understand another point of view or piece of information with a sincere intent to learn doesn't compromise us, it simply makes us more informed. Contempt is not a virtue.

Further Perspectives on Communicating with God

Thus far, we've determined that God is always speaking to us, sending the truths of eternity, and we must seek to "hear Him" by believing, exercising faith, and having a singleness of mind and heart to His will. There remain other questions about our communication with God, the source of all truth, that still come to mind for me. A few of these include: How does God hear my prayers? How quickly does He hear and answer? What if I don't hear Him in words to my ears or to my mind?

Let's walk through a chain of scriptures that has become meaningful to me when I consider some of these questions. I'll provide comments between each of the scriptures, but in case you'd like to explore the chain on your own first, it is: Alma 9:26 → Isaiah 65:24 → Isaiah 55:8–9 → Mosiah 4:9 → 3 Nephi 19:31–34 → Alma 32:35. Here's the first scripture:

> And not many days hence the Son of God shall come in his glory; and his glory shall be the glory of the Only Begotten of the Father, full of grace, equity, and truth, full of patience, mercy, and long-suffering, quick to hear the cries of his people and to answer their prayers. (Alma 9:26)

This verse provides such a beautiful description of the love of our Savior. If your picture of God listening to your prayers ever needs to be refreshed, please consider these adjectives to remind yourself Whom you're petitioning. Dismiss all parts of any image of an impatient or frustrated listener! No matter how far we stray or how senseless our requests, He is "full of grace, equity, and truth, full of patience, mercy, and long-suffering" (Alma 9:26). Just as we discussed in the previous chapter: *know Whom you're communicating with.* Also, since He says

He is quick to hear our prayers, I have to ask: How quick is *quick*? That brings us to the next verse:

> And it shall come to pass, that before they call, I will answer;
> and while they are yet speaking, I will hear. (Isaiah 65:24)

Let this verse sink in. Put it in the context of all we have discussed about God always speaking and the truths of eternity being available for those who tune in to them. Even in times when it seems heaven is silent, if we are petitioning the Lord and striving to hear the Spirit, then we may consider amplifying our confidence that He is there, speaking, and guiding us, even if we do not recognize the particular mechanism for how He is doing so. *Before* we call, He has already answered.* This really speaks to the omniscience and foreknowledge of God. It also adds weight to inspired scripture written thousands of years earlier but intended specifically for our day. It is quite possible that the answers we seek only need to be discovered, not newly received. The Savior's words come to mind here: "your Father knoweth what things ye have need of, before ye ask him" (Matthew 6:8). Notice also that we did get an answer to how "quickly" God will hear our prayers: Immediately, or as we are "yet speaking." Next verse:

> For my thoughts are not your thoughts, neither are your ways
> my ways, saith the Lord.

---

* There's a fascinating tie-in with light here. According to the theory of relativity, the speed of light is constant when measured from any point of observation. This means that if a person traveling on a rocket ship turns on a flashlight, and a person standing on the earth measures the speed of the light coming from the flashlight, it will be the same as the speed of light measured by the person holding the flashlight. How is this possible? Because time and distance will dilate to keep the speed of light constant from the perspective of any observer. This means that while it may take about eight minutes (Earth time) for photons of light to travel from the sun to the earth, if you were traveling on the light itself (at the speed of light), the trip would be instantaneous. Consider how "Before they call, I will answer" (Isaiah 65:24) could be understood in conjunction with "God is light" (1 John 1:5) and "whatsoever is truth is light" (Doctrine and Covenants 84:45).

For as the heavens are higher than the earth, so are my ways higher than your ways, and my thoughts than your thoughts. (Isaiah 55:8–9)

This reminds us that there are boundaries in our ability to understand how communication with God works. To me, the most important takeaway from these verses is not that God works in ways we cannot fully grasp, but rather that we shouldn't assume we're able to predict or explain all the ways God *will* communicate. If we get too focused on receiving a certain feeling, thought, or other impact, we may miss the countless other ways the Spirit is communicating with us. There are times when we may knock on one door and the result is a different door opening—the knocking was still effective at opening the Lord's intended way for us, but not if we continue to stand in front of the still-closed door waiting for *it* to open.* Again, His ways are higher and thus often different than our ways. The next verse cements this further and brings us back to the foundational requirements for being prepared to hear Him:

Believe in God; believe that he is, and that he created all things, both in heaven and in earth; believe that he has all wisdom, and all power, both in heaven and in earth; believe that man doth not comprehend all the things which the Lord can comprehend. (Mosiah 4:9)

Isn't it interesting that we need to *believe that we're not able to comprehend everything*? While this statement clearly dictates a strong need for humility, it also points to the generous and long-suffering God just

---

* This is a reference to the oft-used phrase in scripture to "knock, and it shall be opened unto you," which typically appears in conjunction with "ask, and ye shall receive" (see, e.g., Doctrine and Covenants 4:7 or Matthew 7:7). My use of this example is not to suggest that God *only* gives us what we don't anticipate; rather, that He will give us what we most need according to His infinite wisdom and perfect love. Consider the full teaching from Jesus in Matthew 7:7–12, making clear that God knows how to give the very best "gifts," in the grand scheme of things, he gives what is far better than what we may have specifically asked for.

discussed, who understands the constraints of mortality and offers us tremendous grace when we don't comprehend all things—there's no expectation we will. It's also a great reminder that belief in God, and all He has done and can do, is the currency for exchanging communication with heaven. This reinforces that God's power is far beyond what we can comprehend, so we shouldn't limit how He may communicate. But there's one additional point here: We must also be careful not to limit what it is God will communicate. In other words, it's not just openness to *how* He speaks to us but *what* He will say that's needed. We're reminded He has all wisdom and all power, not just on Earth but also in heaven—an expanse we can't even fathom! We must yield ourselves entirely to His wisdom, with no blindness of mind, if we want to increase our capacity to receive the truths He's sending.

This next verse provides one of the most touching examples of how God's communications with us may not follow any means or mechanism we can describe. This comes from Jesus's visit among the Nephites:

> And it came to pass that [Jesus] went again a little way off and prayed unto the Father;
>
> And tongue cannot speak the words which he prayed, neither can be written by man the words which he prayed.
>
> And the multitude did hear and do bear record; and their hearts were open and they did understand in their hearts the words which he prayed.
>
> Nevertheless, so great and marvelous were the words which he prayed that they cannot be written, neither can they be uttered by man. (3 Nephi 19:31–34)

Just as the Nephites experience in Jesus's presence, the most divine communications cannot be spoken, heard, or written—they can only be understood in the heart (when the Holy Spirit communicates directly to our spirit). I love that some people hear audible words from God in answer to their prayers. I love that others hear a voice in their minds. But what I love maybe even more is that some know God is speaking to them even if they hear no voice and sense no specific words. Note, the Nephites *were not* forbidden to write the words; they simply *could not* write them. I think of this as the type of communication from God that we struggle to put into words—there's something about the purity of the impact it has on our souls that defies description. Often, I believe we translate such divine communications into phrases like "the Spirit spoke to me" or "words came to my mind," even though the true source was far deeper and beyond description. President Boyd K. Packer taught that "even though it is described as a voice," the Spirit "is a voice that one feels, more than one hears."[4] This brings us to our last verse:

> O then, is not this real? I say unto you, Yea, because it is light; and whatsoever is light, is good, because it is discernible, therefore ye must know that it is good; and now behold, after ye have tasted this light is your knowledge perfect? (Alma 32:35)

We're pulling this out of its rich and detailed context of Alma 32, but it's still relevant here. What you have experienced in communication from God absolutely is real, even if it goes beyond description! Alma tries to explain it as a seed growing up to a tree of life within your soul, complete with "swelling motions" (Alma 32:28) and expansion of the mind (see Alma 32:34). The question that begins this verse can be rhetorical—of course it's real, of course it's good, because it's light, and it brings greater discernment, just as visible light does for our vision! We may not be able to explain exactly what's happening in our soul when God is communicating with us, but we can be assured that it's real, and as we nourish it, the light will "[grow] brighter and brighter until the perfect day" (Doctrine and Covenants 50:24). That day is one when we "chase darkness from among [us]" (50:25) and "[know] all things" (93:28).

Let's close out this discussion with an excellent analogy and instruction from Elder Kyle S. McKay:

> Answers from God in response to earnest inquiries come by the power of the Holy Ghost, speaking to your mind and to your heart—your spiritual sense of learning. Trying to understand the things of God by some way other than the Spirit of God is like trying to understand the flavor of food by listening to it. You're using the wrong sense! If we neglect our *spiritual* sense of learning and feeling, we will never adequately know God's truth. In fact, without the Spirit of God, the things of God will probably seem foolish. Paul confirmed, "The natural man receiveth not the things of the Spirit of God: for they are foolishness unto him: neither can he know them, because they are spiritually discerned."
>
> The language of the Spirit has been described as "original but inarticulate, heard only with the soul." Without some level of fluency in the language of the Spirit, you cannot know the foundational truths you must know so that you cannot fall. I urge you to become acquainted with and fluent in the language of the Spirit.[5]

Fluency in the language of the Spirit is something that comes easier for some than others. Regardless of where you may place yourself on the fluency spectrum, I hope you can increase your confidence that God is, in fact, lovingly listening and constantly communicating with you.

Applying the Principles

1. **Prioritize prayer:** Regular, sincere prayer is essential in maintaining a connection with God, the ultimate source of all truth. Make it a priority in your daily life. Know that our loving Heavenly Father instantly hears and has already answered all your pleas with patience, long-suffering, and mercy. Prayer is a conversation worth having,

again and again, as it deepens your relationship with God and opens your heart to His guidance.

2. **Let the Holy Spirit be your guide:** Actively seek personal revelation through prayer, scripture study, and temple worship. Be patient and attentive to the promptings of the Spirit, trusting that guidance is coming and may become clearer as you strive to be worthy and receptive. The Holy Spirit's influence is crucial in navigating life's complexities and making decisions aligned with God's will. Above all, it's worth it to rely on the Spirit by *believing* He's working in us, not limiting *how* by expecting certain feelings or thoughts, but by embracing through trust in God that His ways are higher than ours.

3. **Trust in God's timing:** Revelation and understanding may not be obvious to us immediately. This doesn't mean God isn't communicating or working with us. Our reception and appreciation of certain truths may be increased by God's use of delayed insight or divine silence. Trust in God's timing and continue to seek His guidance with faith and humility. Remember, His ways are not our ways; they are higher and holier. Just as He's perfectly patient with us, so should we strive for patience with His omniscient timing, trusting that His answers will be understood when they're most needed and most beneficial.

In this journey to find what is true in a world of confusion, our connection to and communication with the Source of all truth must be protected and strengthened. As the quote at the heading of this chapter vividly illustrates, without dependence on the truths available from God we would be left in the gutter of mass information without taking advantage of the glorious view of the stars that's available.

Reflecting back on my tour at Versailles provides a metaphorical connection to our own seeking of greater comprehension in this life.

We are all here on a "tour" of mortality, and the Lord has provided us with "the Spirit of truth [who] will guide [us] into all truth" (John 16:13). Will we take the Holy Spirit to be our guide? Will we yield ourselves to God's will, with an eye single to His glory and a mind single to Him, to become true receivers of His eternal truths? Blindness of mind will invariably harden our hearts and compromise access to our Heavenly Guide. We should truly:

> *Let the Holy Spirit guide;*
> *Let him teach us what is true.*
> *He will testify of Christ,*
> *Light our minds with heaven's view.*[6]

Chapter 8

KNOW FOR YOURSELF

It's not what you look at that matters, it's what you see.
—Unknown

You know how some phrases are emblematic of a certain time in your life? One phrase that instantly takes me back to elementary school is: "Prove it!" The exclamation point is crucial, because this was almost always shouted at an elevated volume to challenge someone's bold claim. "I can climb to the top of the swing set," "My parents own a limousine," or "My dog weighs 400 pounds" are the types of remarks that would be met with a forceful "Prove it!" I'm sure it comes as no surprise that the demanded evidence was rarely provided, or when it was, disaster often followed. Poor Mikey and that nasty fall he took from near the top of the playground swing set. Ouch.

Despite the childish memories it conjures for me, this demand for proof of a claim aligns with the motto of the oldest continuously existing scientific academy in the world: The Royal Society of London for Improving Natural Knowledge (also known as the United Kingdom's national academy of sciences). Their motto, *nullius in verba*, which adorns the coat of arms of the Royal Society, means "take nobody's word for it." The Royal Society's website explains that the motto is "an expression of the determination of Fellows to withstand the domination of authority and to verify all statements by an appeal to facts determined by experiment."[1]

In the cases of science and invention (and perhaps even in playground antics), *nullius in verba* can serve as an effective guiding principle. I often tell PhD students in my research lab that the most important result is not the initial, game-changing data point; it's the *reproduction* of that data point. This is essential not only for our own experiments as part of scientific rigor and reproducibility but also for verifying findings reported by others.

An example of *nullius in verba* in action is when the Wright brothers, Wilbur and Orville, were carrying out their early glider experiments in 1900 and 1901. Their glider designs had relied on aerodynamic data, such as lift tables developed by Otto Lilienthal, which were widely regarded as authoritative at the time. However, the gliders were not performing as expected and the brothers questioned the data from which they'd generated their designs. At length, they decided to conduct their own experiments, including constructing a wind tunnel in their bicycle shop in Dayton, Ohio, to test various wing shapes and configurations. They generated entirely new lift tables along with additional data at greater precision than had previously been accessible. Through their experiments, they discovered that the Smeaton coefficient, used in calculating lift and drag, was incorrect in the previously reported tables. Use of their newly developed coefficient and corresponding tables led to the successful design of the 1902 glider and the historic 1903 Wright Flyer, which enabled the first powered flight.[2]

While the Wright brothers' experience exemplifies the importance of *nullius in verba*, the idea of questioning everything reported by others has its limits. We simply wouldn't have made the scientific and technological progress of the past few centuries if we didn't rely on the reported findings of others. As a matter of fact, there isn't a reputable scientific journal in the world that would publish a paper that didn't cite the foundational or related work of others on which the presented research was based. Surely a practitioner of modern electronics is not expected to revisit and perform all the foundational experiments that led to the discovery of semiconductors and the launch of the digital era. At some point, sufficient reproduction and validation of reported data establishes it as accepted fact—or truth.

What about when it comes to knowledge of gospel truth? Is *nullius in verba* an advisable strategy for identifying and embracing gospel truths? If not, where is the boundary between what should be tested for ourselves and what should be embraced based on the preponderance of evidence? In exploring these questions, one aspect of securing our own knowledge of gospel truths becomes very clear: the process is not the same as with scientific truth. No matter how much we may want things to be formulaic, the Lord's communication to us in confirming truth is too personal, too individualistic, to be captured in one simplified universal equation. It's precisely this individual nature of the confirming witnesses of gospel truth that makes *knowing* an incredibly personal process.

Why the "Experiment on the Word" Is Not a Scientific Experiment

When Alma is teaching the Zoramites in Alma 32, he provides one of the most compelling and visual descriptions of coming to know gospel truth. He headlines his description with the invitation to "awake and arouse your faculties, even to an experiment upon my words" (Alma 32:27). Use of the word "experiment" in this verse (along with two other instances in the chapter) has led many to take what Alma is proposing here to be formulaic in a scientific fashion. Scientifically, with an experiment designed to test a hypothesis, there's exclusive dependence on observation and reason. This would be an incomplete approach to finding gospel truth, as it's missing a key catalytic ingredient: faith! As Alma says after calling this an experiment, "Exercise a particle of faith, yea, even if ye can no more than desire to believe, let this desire work in you, even until ye believe in a manner that ye can give place for a portion of my words" (Alma 32:27).

This would be terrible science. To begin a scientific experiment when you've already decided to believe in a particular outcome violates the nature of the scientific process. A hypothesis may postulate what's expected, but it must be tested with absolute openness to whatever the result may be. In other words, it's observation and reason without faith.

Elder Dale G. Renlund taught that discovering gospel truth requires the collective function of observation, reason, and faith:

> Brothers and sisters, we blunder if we equate this experiment [in Alma 32] to the scientific method, even though it uses observation and reasoning. A scientific experiment carefully seeks to minimize—or, preferably, eliminate—inclinations toward a particular outcome. Skepticism is a treasured attribute when using the scientific method and is necessary to interpret the results correctly.
>
> The experiment encouraged by Alma was different; a favorable outcome depended on an inclination to believe. . . .
>
> Alma recommended that his listeners abandon skepticism and encouraged an inclination to believe. He even counseled against approaching the experiment neutrally so that they didn't accidentally "cast [the seed] out by [their] unbelief." . . .
>
> When we start with an inclination to believe, observation leads to faith. As faith grows, reason facilitates the transformation of faith into revelatory knowledge, and revelatory knowledge produces added faith.[3]

He went on to explain that the seed Alma instructed the Zoramites to plant in their hearts was the Son of God, that they "begin to believe . . . he will come to redeem his people, and that he shall suffer and die to atone for their sins; and that he shall rise again from the dead, which shall bring to pass the resurrection" (Alma 33:22). This truth, the reality of the Savior Jesus Christ and His Atonement, is the very core of all gospel truth—the glue that holds all others together.

Step One: Believe

Just as the methodologies for finding truth about fish differed for the two fish scientists in the parable of Chapter 2, so does this fundamental step in finding gospel truth differ from that of the scientific process. Another example of this (to add to that of Alma's sermon to the Zoramites in Alma 32) is found in the oft-quoted promise at the end of the Book of Mormon:

> And when ye shall receive these things, I would exhort you that ye would ask God, the Eternal Father, in the name of Christ, *if these things are **not** true*; and if ye shall ask with a sincere heart, with real intent, having faith in Christ, he will manifest the truth of it unto you, by the power of the Holy Ghost. (Moroni 10:4; emphasis added)

Why is the word "not" present in this invitation? Why wouldn't we ask if the Book of Mormon *is* true—isn't that what we're seeking to determine? I thought about this often on my mission, particularly as I witnessed so many people tell me they'd tried to follow the process and didn't receive an answer. Of course, I cannot unpack all the reasons why that conclusion was reached, as each person had their own distinct circumstances and background. However, there's one key ingredient that was potentially missing: faith.

The promise found in Moroni 10, which is shared with virtually anyone that missionaries give a Book of Mormon to, is often interpreted as scientifically formulaic:

Read + Ponder + Ask God = Manifestation of truth

While this contains some true principles, the simplicity of their combination could be misleading. Don't get me wrong, some may look at this and say, "That's what I did, and I received a witness of the truth from the Holy Ghost!" That's terrific, but we needn't panic if it wasn't our experience. For some who run this "experiment," the result is negative or, at best, null. A probable reason for this is taught by the same prophet who wrote this promise, Moroni:

> But he that *believeth these things* which I have spoken, *him will I visit with the manifestations of my Spirit,* and he shall know and bear record. For because of my Spirit he shall know that these things are true; for it persuadeth men to do good. (Ether 4:11; emphasis added)

It is the absence of choosing to believe that often leaves so many reactions incomplete when they seek to follow the initial formula above. You may think I could just rewrite the formula with a "+ believe it is true" on the left-hand side; but I will not. I've decidedly moved away from being too formulaic when it comes to receiving personal witnesses of gospel truth. Following the suggested steps is always encouraged, but the most important element doesn't fit neatly or isn't sufficiently weighted in a simple formula: complete dependence on God and belief in Him. This draws back to two of the three overarching principles from this book (see Chapter 1): God is the ultimate source of truth, and we must choose to believe.

Witnesses and the *Rashomon* Effect

An important component of choosing to believe something is determining how much dependence we should have on the witness of others. Arriving at a place where we can "give place for a portion" of the word of God (Alma 32:27) often requires embracing the witness of someone we trust. This person could be a full-time missionary who gives us a copy of the Book of Mormon or a family member who shares their personal experience of finding gospel truth or a Church leader who powerfully testifies of God's ability to lead us to truth. Whatever the source, this initial extension of trust in the word of another is virtually always a part of establishing our initial belief (see Romans 10:14).

While it's clear that witnesses are important for establishing belief, we should diligently seek for our own confirmation—to know for ourselves. Ultimately, overdependence on the word of others can be an unstable foundation of faith when the storms of adversity rage. The fact is, you're going to have people from many different perspectives and convictions cross your path in life. When information presented as truth from those people does not align with what you've come to believe and know, what will you do? If you remain dependent only on the word of others, it's likely the pressures of opposition to that truth will present as a "mist of darkness" causing you to "lose [your] way" (1 Nephi 8:23).

One of the hazards to be aware of when it comes to the word of others is the *Rashomon* effect. This effect generally refers to when the same event is recounted by several eyewitnesses whose stories differ in irreconcilable ways. The origin of this term is a 1950 Japanese film directed by Akira Kurosawa titled *Rashomon*, in which a murder is described by four eyewitnesses, each with wildly different stories. The film is considered a landmark in cinematic storytelling, and you've likely seen its namesake effect used in many other films, shows, or stories.* For instance, sitcom comedies like to employ the *Rashomon* effect to demonstrate the often-humorous unreliability of different eyewitnesses retelling the same event. I remember this being used frequently in the show *Family Matters*, where the resident nerd, Steve Urkel, would have a very different version of events to tell than the members of the Winslow family he frequently pestered. It's a great comedy technique! A more recent example is in the famous musical *Hamilton*, where sisters

---

* You can find a list of examples from various forms of media at *TVTropes.org* (website) under the heading *"Rashomon"*-Style; available at https://tvtropes.org/pmwiki/pmwiki .php/Main/RashomonStyle; accessed 4 November 2024.

Eliza and Angelica Schuyler have back-to-back solos ("Helpless" and "Satisfied") recounting the night they met Alexander Hamilton and the events leading up to his wedding to Eliza. In between the two songs, there's a brilliant stage rewind effect used to emphasize the return to the same story told from a different perspective.

We shouldn't overlook the four gospels of the New Testament as another example of the *Rashomon* effect. Each gospel is written by a separate witness, and some events are described with significant differences. Some of these distinctions can be argued as relating to the various intended audiences for each gospel (e.g., Matthew to the Jews, Luke to the Gentiles). Yet there are still details that don't line up—does this mean the gospels aren't "true," or that they don't lead a person to the truth? No, it doesn't, because the central purpose and truth of the gospels is not in their timeline or the logistical details of events, but in their witness of Jesus Christ's divinity and their invitation to follow Him. In a way, the differences in secondary details with overarching consistency in the most important points gives credibility to the various narratives.

Can you think of instances when you have experienced the *Rashomon* effect in your life? This is actually a humorous and favorite pastime for my wife and me—we love retelling the same event from our own viewpoint! I don't think we're alone in this, right? Just ask any married couple to tell the story of how they met or got engaged and *poof!*—instant *Rashomon* effect.

Not too long ago, I was playing chess on the Chess.com app against my teenage son Grant, who's unquestionably a better chess player than I am. As the endgame was winding down, I thought, *I'm playing some amazing chess here!* A few moves later, the game ended in a satisfying draw. I was still smiling over my success when Grant texted, "That was probably the worst game I've ever played." It was the same game, played from different sides, with totally different views of how it went. (Obviously, it was a rare demonstration of my true chess master talent!)

What does the *Rashomon* effect tell us about spiritual things, particularly about finding truth? At least three things:

- Don't allow how others perceive or experience things to negate your own personal experience. Only *you* know what you experienced; don't let others take that from you. Think of the quote at the beginning of this chapter—it's not what you *look at*; it's what you *see* that matters. Many people can look at the same scene and see very different things.
- Don't take from others the things they may have experienced differently from you. I was in a Sunday School class many years ago that I didn't feel was very engaging. As my mind wandered, the sister sitting in front of me handed her fussy baby to her husband and said, "Will you take her? I don't want to miss this!" Clearly we were having totally different experiences even though we were sitting in the same room. My lack of spiritual engagement shouldn't suggest a lack of opportunity to be spiritually engaged.
- Historians would say the more eyewitnesses the better. And the more those witnesses agree, the better. This becomes important with key events of the Restoration, which have strong, consistent eyewitness support (that is, little to no *Rashomon* effect).

Too often, I feel like personal confirmations of the truthfulness of the gospel are abandoned when someone is told by another that their experience was different. It's not even the typical *Rashomon* effect, but rather a different person's telling of what is assumed to be a similar experience: one of testimony-supporting evidences. Just because someone else has stepped away from the conviction they once held for the truthfulness of the gospel, does not mean your evidence and knowledge should be diminished! I know, it's easier said than done, but perhaps pointing this out will help in preparing you against such challenges in the future.

As the prophet Enos noted about his witness from God, "I, Enos, knew that God could not lie" (Enos 1:6). God has provided you with the evidence of truth you've received, in whatever form it's come to you—don't allow the perspective of another to compromise your belief in that truth. If you've experienced something truly transformative, you should record it and apply the same stamp of approval as Enos: you know God cannot lie, and He has spoken to you!* The Prophet Joseph Smith experienced great turmoil about this, even though he was the only one who truly knew what happened in the woods that spring morning of 1820. He said:

> Though I was hated and persecuted for saying that I had seen a vision, yet it was true; . . . Why persecute me for telling the truth? I have actually seen a vision; and who am I that I can withstand God, or why does the world think to make me deny what I have actually seen? For I had seen a vision; *I knew it, and I knew that God knew it*, and I could not deny it, neither dared I do it; at least I knew that by so doing I would offend God, and come under condemnation. (Joseph Smith—History 1:25; emphasis added)

Joseph's firsthand witness with the First Vision brings up another important aspect of coming to know the truthfulness of the gospel for ourselves: Truth cannot be relative.

---

* Elder Neil L. Andersen referred to these as "spiritually defining memories" in his April 2020 general conference talk. He taught: "Embrace your sacred memories. Believe them. Write them down. Share them with your family. Trust that they come to you from your Heavenly Father and His Beloved Son. Let them bring patience to your doubts and understanding to your difficulties." Neil L. Andersen, "Spiritually Defining Memories," *Ensign*, May 2020.

Can Truth Be Relative?

My mother-in-law has often shared an insightful story about how sometimes what's intended is not exactly what's received when we communicate. Her story is that a woman attended a session at the temple, and as she was moving between rooms as part of the ordinance, one of the temple workers whispered to her, "Please, don't you come again." She was taken aback by this comment and asked, "What did you say?" The temple worker repeated, "Please, don't you come again." Still shocked to be told something so rude while in the temple, she inquired one more time what the worker was saying to her. Finally, the temple worker slowly and deliberately enunciated, "*Please. Don't. Chew. Gum. Again.*" Maybe not the most appropriate or helpful thing to say to someone worshipping in the temple, but certainly a far cry from what the woman heard initially!

You've likely had something like this happen, right? Where the intended meaning of something is completely misconstrued? Not intentionally, but by misunderstanding, lack of context, or improper assumptions. Without asking for clarification, the woman would have had a very different story to tell. Rather than one that ended with the reveal of a humorous misunderstanding, it could have been an example of being treated rudely by a temple worker or being perceived as unworthy or unwanted—the *Rashomon* effect at work without either party even realizing it. This reminds us that truth is truth, but interpretation is subjective and based on understanding and myriad other factors.

While our level of confidence or belief in something may be relative, the truth regarding that thing cannot be relative. It *is*, or it *is not*. When we know something, we know it. To have someone proclaim that something is one way does not make it that way. Consider the counsel from President Russell M. Nelson on this topic:

The adversary has . . . disturbing tactics. Among them are his efforts to blur the line between what is true and what is not true. The flood of information available at our fingertips, ironically, makes it increasingly difficult to determine what is true . . .

Dear brothers and sisters, God is the source of all truth. The Church of Jesus Christ of Latter-day Saints embraces *all* truth that God conveys to His children, whether learned in a scientific laboratory or received by direct revelation from Him.[4]

President Nelson's comment about the blurring of the line between what is true and what is not true is a powerful one. When it comes to gospel truth, the promise is you can gain knowledge that "is perfect in that thing . . . because you know, for ye know that the word hath swelled your souls, and ye also know that it hath sprouted up, that your understanding doth begin to be enlightened, and your mind doth begin to expand" (Alma 32:34). Notice, it's not once you're fully enlightened or when your mind is completely expanded and you comprehend *everything*; it's when you notice the *beginning* of these that you know the seed is good, and the thing is true.

Observing and Reasoning That the Seed Is Good

We've established that gaining a personal knowledge of gospel truth requires observation, reason, and faith. The process demands choosing to believe—it's the catalyst or prerequisite—which typically is enabled by trusting in the word of a witness. We then considered various aspects of witnesses, with the most important witness being ourselves. Finally, the truthfulness of something is not relative—it's either true or it's not.

What happens next should be the personal witness or confirmation from the Holy Spirit. This is the moment Alma identified as knowing the "seed is good; for behold it swelleth, and sprouteth, and beginneth to grow" (Alma 32:30). This experience will vary greatly from person to person, as it's uniquely tailored to your soul. Just as a tree growing in a specific environment pushes down roots and extends branches according to the soil quality, available space, and surrounding objects, so too will your testimony develop in a way that is suited to your individual circumstances.

Let's review a few examples from the scriptures where people recognized that the seed they planted was good. In some instances, this relates directly to conversion and the initial spark of testimony; in others, it involves ongoing revelation that deepens their understanding of truth. As you read these likely familiar examples, reflect on your own experiences when you've observed a gospel teaching faithfully planted in your soul and recognized the evidence of it being a good seed.

- **Lamanites not knowing they knew.** At a time in the Book of Mormon when many Lamanites repented and were converted to the Lord, we learn that they had not realized the depth of their conversion. The Savior says, "whoso cometh unto me with a broken heart and a contrite spirit, him will I baptize with fire and with the Holy Ghost, even as the Lamanites, because of their faith in me at the time of their conversion, were baptized with fire and with the Holy Ghost, and they knew it not" (3 Nephi 9:20). Perhaps you've had spiritual experiences that were difficult to recognize as personal confirmations when they happened, but looking back on them allows you to see that the divine power of God was at work for you.

- **Hindsight confirmation on the road to Emmaus.** Speaking of how we may have to look back on experiences to recognize the growth of a good seed or experience, there may be no better example than the two disciples of Jesus who were traveling to Emmaus not long after His crucifixion. They had unknowingly walked with the resurrected Lord, talked with

Him, and ate with Him, until finally "their eyes were opened, and they knew him; and he vanished out of their sight" (Luke 24:31). Once the Lord had gone, they reflected on the hours spent with Him, and said to each other, "Did not our heart burn within us, while he talked with us by the way, and while he opened to us the scriptures?" (24:32).

- **Seeking the Lord's aid for any unbelief.** In one of the most touching interchanges in all of scripture, a father brings his tormented child to Jesus for healing. After taking inventory of the situation, Jesus said to the boy's father, "If thou canst believe, all things are possible to him that believeth" (Mark 9:23). Straightaway the father cried out "and said with tears, Lord, I believe; help thou mine unbelief" (9:24). Regarding this man, Elder David A. Bednar taught:

> I wonder if the intent of the man's pleading was not primarily to help him believe in Jesus as our Redeemer and in His healing power. He already may have acknowledged Christ as the Son of God. But perhaps he needed help to believe the Master's healing power indeed could be so individual and so personalized as to bless his own beloved son. He may have believed in Christ generally but not believed Christ specifically and personally.
>
> We often testify of what we know to be true, but perhaps the more relevant question for each of us is whether we believe what we know.[5]

- **Gradual revelation or understanding for Peter.** Even though he was the prophet of the Lord's church, Peter did not necessarily receive revelation with clear, immediate understanding. In Acts 10, he has an elaborate vision with imagery of a descending vessel, large sheet, food, and so forth. He didn't understand what it meant and "while Peter thought on the vision, the Spirit said unto him, Behold, three men seek thee. Arise therefore, and get thee down, and go with them, doubting nothing: for I have sent them" (Acts 10:19–20). I love how the Spirit speaks clearly to Peter with the instructions to meet these men but did not simply speak clearly to him the meaning of the vision! Remember, the Lord's ways are not our ways (see Isaiah 55:8–9). The men ended up leading Peter to meet with a Gentile, and the experience taught Peter the meaning of his vision. This isn't a stand-alone instance where God teaches by showing rather than telling (see, for example, 1 Nephi 11).

- **Just knowing one truth and holding to it.** My favorite story in the New Testament is of the man who was born blind as recorded in John 9. Jesus heals the man, who then finds himself brought before the intimidating Pharisees. Their interrogation confirms what they'd heard: Jesus had healed this man on the Sabbath. So they instruct the man, "Give God the praise: we know that [Jesus] is a sinner" (John 9:24). At this point, this man, who'd lived his entire life without sight until only days (perhaps hours?) before this meeting, says back to them in simple honesty, "Whether [Jesus] be a sinner or no, I know not: one thing I know, that, whereas I was blind, now I see" (9:25). Just one truth. I love that! Granted, it was a major thing to have known and experienced, but so also was the intensity of pressure and rebuke coming from the leading religious figures of the day! Nothing was going to unmoor this man from his one truth, even if prominent dignitaries of his time told him otherwise. Ultimately, Jesus found the man, who'd been cast out of the synagogue, and revealed Himself to him. Jesus will always find us.

These are just a few examples of having personal confirmation of gospel truth via communication from God. I hope this helps to show that every person's path may look a little different, but there's a common theme: When we choose to believe and act in faith, God will be there to answer with knowledge, in His own time and His own way.

Applying the Principles

1. **Balance skepticism with faith:** *Nullius in verba*, "take nobody's word for it," can be a useful guiding principle in scientific inquiry, but it has important limitations. A broader modern equivalent is "question everything"—while compelling in principle, if exclusively embraced, it can lead to excessive doubt, even about absolute and core truths. Recognize the need for balance in your search for truth, allowing room for both questioning and faith.

2. **Combine observation, reason, and faith:** Receiving a personal confirmation of gospel truth requires a combination of observation, reason, and faith—where faith requires choosing to believe. If any one of these is missing, it compromises your readiness to receive and recognize spiritual confirmations. Consider how you might help others understand the importance of belief when it comes to gaining a personal confirmation of the truthfulness of the Book of Mormon or other gospel truths.

3. **Understand the *Rashomon* effect:** Be aware of the *Rashomon* effect, where different people may interpret the same event differently. Don't allow others' perspectives to undermine what you personally see, feel, and know. Remember, God cannot lie, and the witness you've received comes from Him. Trust in that divine confirmation above the varying opinions of others.

4. **Acknowledge the absoluteness of truth:** Truth isn't relative—something either happened or it didn't; a gospel principle is either

true or it isn't. You can gain a perfect knowledge of the truthfulness of these things by conducting the "experiment" described in Alma 32, which involves personalized application of observation, reason, and faith.

5. **Be open to diverse communications from God:** The Lord provides confirming witnesses of gospel truth in many ways. The scriptures contain numerous examples of these when people are able to recognize the "seed is good" based on what's able to grow. Be open to the unique ways the Lord may choose to confirm truth to you, from a distinct voice or sign to a noticeable change in perspective or disposition (see Mosiah 5:2). Trust in the Lord, and do not limit the methods by which He will witness truth to you. You *can* know for yourself.

6. **Share your testimony:** As you gain your own confirmation of gospel truths, consider how you can share your testimony with others. Your experiences can help others in their own journey of faith, providing support and encouragement as they seek their own confirmations.

Just like the demands to "prove it!" shouted on my elementary school playground, you may find yourself needing to convincingly demonstrate how you know the gospel is true. Some of the pressure may come from others who have passed through similar things as you but see them very differently—the *Rashomon* effect. Then again, the toughest pressure may not come from them, but from within. By collectively applying observation, reason, and faith, you will be enlightened and receive a definitive personal witness of the truth. This witness will be personal in its distinctness from any other witness, for it's from God to you. Trust in this witness and add further confirmations to it as you press forward on the covenant path.

Chapter 9

BUT HOW DO I *KNOW* I KNOW?

We often testify of what we know to be true, but
perhaps the more relevant question for each of us is
whether we believe what we know.

—Elder David A. Bednar

My first exposure to scientific research came in the form of a summer internship at Purdue University in 2004. It was the last summer of my undergrad, and a friend of mine had piqued my interest in the booming field of nanotechnology. The project I was recruited to work on involved the use of a plasma-enhanced chemical vapor deposition (PECVD) tool to grow carbon nanotubes (CNTs). If you haven't heard of PECVD or CNTs before this moment, then you're basically in the same boat I was before that summer began!

Thankfully, I had excellent mentorship from a PhD student in the research group where I was working. Within a few weeks, I learned how the PECVD tool worked, what carbon nanotubes were, and why it was important to discover better ways of using PECVD to grow them. Throughout the summer, we were fabricating substrates with different types of catalyst structures—different materials designed with the aim of promoting (in this case) CNT growth. Most of the attempts didn't produce a detectable difference in the subsequent growth, but we meticulously noted the parameters we used and any other relevant conditions we could think of and moved on to the next variation.

One day, everything just worked. We had shifted to a new catalyst support structure on the substrate and carried out the PECVD process consistent with all our previous attempts. When we removed the substrate from the PECVD chamber (once it cooled), the jolt of excitement I felt was indescribable! Typically, the shiny surface of the silicon sample was barely dulled by the presence of a low density of carbon nanotubes. Not for this sample. The shiny surface was completely obscured by a thick, beautiful mat of CNTs—the high absorption of light from the rough film caused it to take on a pure black velvetlike appearance.

We were so excited, we immediately put another of the same catalyst samples into the chamber to try and repeat the growth. A few hours later, we once again were staring at a beautiful high-density growth of carbon nanotubes. In total, we repeated the growth three times that day; the third time we even included a few other types of catalyst substrates in the PECVD in the same growth just to be sure there wasn't something unexpectedly amazing going on with the chamber facilitating this result. Our new catalyst substrate was the only one that came out covered in the dark black CNTs.

Over the ensuing days, we studied the quality and properties of the CNTs that the new catalyst substrates had produced. Given how exciting the results were, we planned out experiments to perform for collecting needed data to write a manuscript for publication in a scientific journal. A few days later, we were back at the PECVD to perform additional growths on a new batch of the substrates. To our shock and utter confusion, when we removed the substrate from the chamber, we found no trace of the dense CNT film. We reviewed the process to figure out what we might have inadvertently changed; we found nothing. So we tried again. And again. And again. Over the remaining weeks of the summer, we tried repeating that growth dozens of times with new batches of substrates, identical conditions, tweaked conditions, even at the same exact time of day (as if that would impact the isolated vacuum chamber of the PECVD). We never could reproduce the growth.

When I returned to the same lab at Purdue for my PhD a year later, I continued to try to reproduce that growth. It wasn't part of my primary PhD project, but over the next few years I would try again and again. The growth never returned. On occasion, I would wonder to myself whether those initial growths had really even happened the way I remembered them. When this thought occurred, I'd dig through the drawer of samples in the lab and reexamine those seemingly magic substrates. Every time, I found that beautiful black forest of CNTs covering the surface in a manner we never could recreate with any similar catalyst structure.

We never did publish the results of those samples; while we'd collected and observed undeniable evidence of the successful CNT growth, repeated across all three samples, we couldn't explain why it wasn't able to be reproduced again. There was something in the process we couldn't understand, and the process would be the most important part of our report to the scientific community. The result or truth we'd uncovered was that the catalyst structure and growth conditions we used were capable of yielding dense CNT growth. But our inability to explain why it could not be replicated suggested there were more variables at play than we were aware of.

This experience with truth from a scientific study has been invaluable in helping me understand how to hold on to core gospel truths I've personally gained a knowledge of through the Spirit. In their initial blossoming within our souls, gospel truths—such as the Atonement of Jesus Christ or the inspired translation of the Book of Mormon—possess a purity and reality that defies description. These are the moments of confirmation from the Spirit of truth that prompt us to declare, "I know," followed by the truths we have discovered for ourselves. However, as time passes, the reproducibility or recurrence of those profound spiritual confirmations may diminish. The vivid memory of what we once experienced can fade, and faith may give way to doubt about things we once knew with certainty. The world pressures us to interpret these lulls as evidence that we never really knew, offering ways to explain away what we experienced.*

When I went through a period like this years ago, I was reminded of my early research experience with growing carbon nanotubes. I recognized the parallels between the thoughts and feelings that overwhelmed me as I repeatedly failed to reproduce the CNT growth. I also reflected on what I did in that situation with the scientific truth—I revisited the reality of the samples. I returned to the lab, saw them, and knew they were real. Even if we, or anyone else, later discovered some other factor in the process that influenced our results that day, it wouldn't change the reality of the truth we had found: CNTs grew on that substrate. Sure, understanding the role of other influences in producing that result would provide valuable context and might even undermine the perceived value of our process in the scientific community, but it doesn't change the results from that day—the truth we came to know.

I realized the same principle can be applied to gospel truths we come to know. I made it a point to revisit the foundational spiritual experiences I've had over the years, allowing myself to honestly reflect on what I observed, felt, and knew with confidence. While I recognized that circumstances, relationships, and environment might have played a role in the *process* when I received a confirming witness that the "seed is good" (Alma 32:30), they do not change the fact that it *is* good! Interestingly, in scientific studies, the process or methods are often what

---

* Jared Halverson describes this as "the fall" in the three stages of our developmental faith, which is composed of: creation, fall, and atonement. He has described this in numerous interviews, including on the *Faith Matters* podcast episode titled, "Don't Let a Good Faith Crisis Go to Waste—Jared Halverson," available at https://faithmatters.org /dont-let-a-good-faith-crisis-go-to-waste-jared-halverson/; accessed 4 November 2024.

matter most, whereas in the gospel, it is the resulting truth we come to know that's most important, with limitless variations in the process based on individual circumstances.†

Just as the CNTs unquestionably grew in the lab that summer day in 2004, so did the gospel seed grow within my soul, leading me to confidently identify it as good. The nature of that seed hasn't changed, nor will it ever, but my confidence or belief in the reality of it being good came into question. Faith trials can happen for any number of reasons. One of the ways is that the pressures of the world and the daily deluge of information cause our hold on gospel truth to slacken. As Elder Bednar so aptly stated in the quote at the beginning of this chapter, the "relevant question for each of us is whether we believe what we know."[1]

Quadrants of Knowledge

There are many studies exploring what it means to know something, a topic of ongoing debate at the heart of the field of epistemology. Not being an expert in this space, my inclinations led me to find different diagrams used to explain the various states of knowledge (I'm sure it comes as no surprise to you at this point I was attracted to diagrams). One such diagram is from educator J. S. Atherton,‡ who divides our state of knowing something into two axes: (1) awareness of self, and (2) knowledge of something. Each of these ranges from not knowing to

---

† I do want to point out a caveat to this. There are instances where the outcome of a spiritual process may teach us less than the process itself. For instance, when a loved one is sick or injured and there are blessings given and faith exercised through fasting and prayer, but then the outcome is not what was desired or anticipated and the person does not get better. It's possible that the process itself provided a strengthening and unification that was more important than the outcome. I'm grateful to a good friend for pointing out this important, alternative perspective to process vs. outcome in spiritual matters.

‡ J. S. Atherton has published his perspective on this in an article titled "Knowing and Not Knowing," *Doceo*; available at https://www.doceo.co.uk/tools/knowing.htm; accessed 5 March 2024.

knowing, but it's not strictly binary, as you could have something at any position between the two extremes. From these two axes, four quadrants are formed, as shown in Figure 18. Let's walk through each of these quadrants.

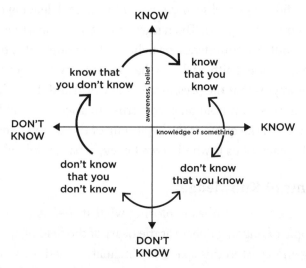

Figure 18. Diagram depicting the quadrants of knowing something. The vertical axis represents our awareness of self and the horizontal axis represents our knowledge of something. There can be data points for specific information all over this grid based on how much we know it (horizontal axis) and how aware we are of knowing it (vertical axis).* Arrows and their corresponding size indicate typical direction things travel between the quadrants.

Not knowing that you don't know

This is what Atherton calls the "ignorance is bliss" quadrant, representative of those who have no idea that they don't know something. This includes those who've never encountered a subject matter and therefore don't even know it exists. Think of the billions of people currently living on Earth with little to no awareness of the restored gospel

---

* Figure is adapted from the article "Knowing and Not Knowing"; available at https://www.doceo.co.uk/tools/knowing.htm.

of Jesus Christ. Also included in this quadrant are many people who express strong positions on topics for which they actually know very little. Their confidence is high, but they don't realize how very little they actually know about the things for which they claim authority. Interest in—or frequent conversation about—something does not bring knowledge of that thing unless we actively put forth the effort to learn. The world is full of people that show great passion for a topic for which all their claims of knowledge and associated arguments to support their position are fallacious. Here are a few examples of common fallacies that show up:[†]

- *Bandwagon fallacy:* Something is true because of who or how many believe it. Example: "The new smartphone model Y is selling out everywhere, so it must be the best smartphone on the market."
- *Causal fallacy:* Something was caused by something else even though their association is weak or nonexistent. Example: "People who own more books tend to have higher incomes, therefore buying more books will make you richer."
- *Strawman fallacy:* Distorting (often by oversimplifying) an opposing viewpoint and then attacking the weaker, inaccurate version. Example: Person A says, "I think it's important to prioritize renewable energy investments." Person B responds, "Person A wants to get rid of all fossil fuels, which is going to cripple our economy!"

Hence, the "not knowing that you don't know" quadrant has many who think they know something but actually do not, largely because the manner in which they've arrived at their perceived knowledge is

---

[†] There are many logical fallacies related to how one expresses (or argues) for their position on a subject. One succinct list of some common ones can be found at https://en.m.wikipedia.org/wiki/List_of_fallacies; accessed 4 November 2024.

fallacious. These are joined by the many who don't know something simply because they've had no opportunity to do so.

Knowing that you don't know

Transitioning from the "not knowing you don't know" quadrant to "knowing you don't know" is very common and comes through exposure to information you previously had no awareness of. There's a need for openness of mind to make this transition. Typically, there's a teacher involved in bringing this awareness to a student. Our time in school should be marked with thousands of transitions between these two quadrants as we gain awareness of so many new things. Yet awareness alone does not bring true knowledge; this quadrant is only where we're aware of something that we don't know. An easy example for me here is most any music-related topic. I know that I don't know how to direct a choir or sing perfectly in tune or read complex scores. For others, an example may be advanced calculus, where you are aware it exists but know that you don't know it.

When it comes to gospel truths, this quadrant represents the things of which we don't yet have a sufficiently convincing personal witness. I see this as the region where Alma began working with the poor among the Zoramites in Alma 32. Those who were "poor as to the things of the world" (Alma 32:3) were cast out of the synagogues and had no place to worship, so they came to Alma and asked, "what shall we do?" (32:5). These people knew they didn't know how to worship God or identify truth from Him, and Alma was going to help them change that. After instructing them regarding the role and importance of humility, Alma encouraged them to exercise faith—to believe in the truth they have received and live it—and they would ultimately come to know for themselves that it is good.

Knowing that you know

Continuing with the Alma 32 example, let's transition to the "knowing that you know" quadrant. This is where you arrive once you observe the seed growing; your observation confirms that the thing is true. You now *know* it. In fact, as Alma says, "your knowledge is perfect in that thing, and your faith is dormant; and this because you know, for ye know that the word hath swelled your souls, and ye also know that it hath sprouted up, that your understanding doth begin to be enlightened, and your mind doth begin to expand" (Alma 32:34). As I've pointed out before, you're not *fully* enlightened, and your mind hasn't expanded to *all* knowledge—it has just begun to expand, and that is the signal of confirmed truthfulness. In secular terms, this is where we move once we've learned something. For example, in my case, I might someday learn how to lead a choir—highly unlikely, but it could happen!

Not knowing that you know

For the "not knowing that you know" quadrant, let's begin with practical knowledge or skills. This is where you find abilities or understandings you might not even realize you possess at a strong level. In one sense, this could be considered an intrinsic talent or skill. A telltale sign of this is when you try to teach the skill to someone else and find it nearly impossible to explain. A compelling example of this is someone who tried to write down a recipe:

> I was once asked to contribute to a cookbook. I have a few recipes which I am quite proud of, and I decided to offer one which involved making a batter. I had to systematize the recipe, and specify quantities: but I just could not get it right. Left to myself, as it were, I could just slurp in the milk and get the right consistency with no problem. I was probably taking account of the size of the egg and several other variables; but for the life of me I could not

specify the quantity of milk. I had the same problem with the herbs in another recipe. I gave up. Interestingly, it was several weeks before I was able to make those recipes again with the same insouciance I had previously taken for granted.[2]

When it comes to gospel truth, it's also possible to not realize that you know. Many people have walked the covenant path for years, enjoying countless fruits of their service and faithfulness, yet they may reach a point where they question whether they've had sufficiently distinct confirmations to *know* for certain the gospel is true. Such a hunt for specific singularities is like losing sight of the forest for the trees—why focus on a few specific trees when you have an entire forest? Someone might be overly concerned with obtaining specific, distinct confirmations of gospel truth (the trees) and, as a result, fail to recognize the broader evidence and experiences that affirm the truthfulness of the gospel as a whole (the forest). The forest is composed of years of enlightenment, an expanded mind, and other fruits all testifying to the truth.

There are also those who fall prey to the pressures of the world and are pulled down to this quadrant of not knowing that they know. These pressures cause them to lose belief in something they have already come to know—they stop believing they know. But does this change the fact that they know it? In many instances it does not. It only changes how they choose to handle that knowledge, leading them to explain away what they previously observed (and reasoned) to be evidence of the truthfulness of those things. This relates to the illusion of truth effect that was mentioned earlier, where repeated exposure to something false can cause someone to embrace it, even though, deep down, they know it's false. Interestingly, a recent study found that individuals falling victim to this fallacy still retain an underlying awareness of what is actually true.[3] This suggests that while repetition can make false statements feel more believable, it doesn't necessarily erase one's deepest inner knowledge of the truth.

I want to be careful to not suggest that gospel truth we have come to know at any point can *never* be un-known. This is based on instruction from the prophet Alma, who teaches that eternal truth can be known by a person who "will not harden [their] heart" until "it is given unto [them] to know the mysteries of God until [they] know them in full" (Alma 12:10). He then provides this warning:

> And they that will harden their hearts, to them is given the lesser portion of the word *until they know nothing concerning his mysteries*; and then they are taken captive by the devil, and led by his will down to destruction. Now this is what is meant by the chains of hell. (Alma 12:11; emphasis added)

There may be different ways to interpret Alma's teachings here, but one reading certainly can be that the word someone once received can be—or will be—taken away; i.e., that which was once known is no longer known. Based on our analysis above, I do think it's possible that something once known still resides within a person, even if it's bound and trapped by the "chains of hell," held "captive by the devil" (Alma 12:11) because of the hardening of someone's heart to the once-known mysteries of God. Elder David P. Homer adds further insight in his October 2024 general conference talk, when he taught:

> At all times, it is helpful to remember Alma's teaching that God gives His word according to the attention and effort we devote to it. If we heed God's word, we will receive more; if we ignore His counsel, we will receive less and less until we have none. This loss of knowledge does not mean that the truth was wrong; rather, it shows that we have lost the capacity to understand it.[*]

---

[*] David P. Homer, "Trusting Our Father," *Liahona*, November 2024. There is a compelling tie-in to our earlier discussion (in Chapter 4) about understanding what we believe. Elder Homer indicates that our loss of knowledge is related to no longer having the capacity to understand what we once knew.

Finally, it's important to acknowledge that some may feel they never have received a confirmation that the gospel seed is good. Perhaps they tried the "experiment" and lived the principles but were left without observed evidence of growth or enlightenment. To anyone that identifies with this, the question to ask is: Do you still desire to believe? If you do, then I encourage you to revisit the approach with as much openness as possible to how and when God will respond. God has promised us that "by the power of the Holy Ghost ye may know the truth of all things" (Moroni 10:5) and that this power comes "according to the faith of the children of men" (10:7). My witness to you is that He *will* respond, providing you with observable evidence that the seed of the gospel is good, so long as you have embraced it with faith and are living according to its truth.

Believing That You Know

Focusing specifically on the truths of the gospel of Jesus Christ, we can consider the vertical axis of Figure 18 as representing belief instead of self-awareness. This adjustment transforms the "not knowing that you know" quadrant into "not believing that you know." This now becomes a space for those who are either drawn away or who willfully choose to disbelieve what they already know—we began discussing some who may fall in this quadrant in the previous section.

Korihor comes to mind here. Despite his adamant declarations against the existence of God, when he was struck dumb, he confessed, "I always knew that there was a God. But behold, the devil hath deceived me" (Alma 30:52–53). He even admits that as he taught the devil's falsehoods as truth, his fame and success led him to "verily [believe] that they were true; and for this cause I withstood the truth" (Alma 30:53). Korihor is evidence that doubting what we know to be true can eventually lead to believing what is not true.* Our four-quadrant diagram represents only things that *are* true and our knowledge of them. To include whether something is true or not would require adding a third dimension (which sounds intriguing, but we'll pass for now). Korihor was dwelling in one of the eight regions of that three-dimensional space.

Bringing it back to the two-dimensional Figure 18 diagram, Amulek is another excellent example of living in a state of not believing that he knew the truthfulness of the gospel. He describes this so perfectly in Alma 10:

> I never have known much of the ways of the Lord, and his mysteries and marvelous power. I said I never had known much of these things; but behold, I mistake, for *I have seen much of his mysteries and his marvelous power*; yea, even in the preservation of the lives of this people.
>
> Nevertheless, I did harden my heart, for I was called many times and I would not hear; therefore *I knew concerning these things, yet I would not know*; therefore I went on rebelling against God, in the wickedness of my heart, even until the fourth day of this seventh month, which is in the tenth year of the reign of the judges. (Alma 10:5–6; emphasis added)

I love how Amulek identifies how he *observed* so many evidences of the truthfulness of the gospel, including the mysteries and marvelous power of God. Yet he chose not to believe, hardening his heart, and thus knowing the truth, but not believing he knew. Something I've always loved about the day he refers to—the day the angel appeared to him and guided him to help Alma—is that it is the fourth day of the seventh

---

* Another effect potentially at work here is what is known as the illusory-truth effect or mere-exposure effect, which explains how people will be more likely to believe something as true simply by being exposed to it excessively.

month; if this had been according to *our* calendar, it would be the fourth of July. In the US, this is Independence Day, which is a day of celebration of our liberties, the origin for which was brought about through the Declaration of Independence on July 4, 1776. In similar fashion, the fourth day of the seventh month on the Nephite calendar was a day of independence for Amulek, as it was the day he chose to believe in what he knew to be true! In his case, it was a truth that "set[s] you free" (John 8:32).

When the signs of Christ's birth appeared to the people in the Americas, including the indisputable night without darkness, all the people witnessed the sign and "began to be astonished because there was no darkness when the night came" (3 Nephi 1:15). Yet, the first lie Satan attempted to spread among the people is that they did *not* see (or should not believe) what they saw:

> And it came to pass that from this time forth there began to be lyings sent forth among the people, by Satan, to harden their hearts, to the intent that they might not believe in those signs and wonders which they had seen; but notwithstanding these lyings and deceivings the more part of the people did believe, and were converted unto the Lord. (3 Nephi 1:22)

If Satan can convince some that they didn't see what they actually saw, he can certainly tempt many more to not believe what they've experienced spiritually. We must each choose to believe and diligently remember what we experience, while choosing to recognize—and not believe—the lies Satan spreads.

Some people struggle with their testimony of the gospel of Jesus Christ and His restored Church because they're not believing what they already know. Remember, it wasn't the visit of an angel that brought evidence of the truth to Amulek—the angel simply motivated him to believe in what he already knew. The evidence and witnesses of that knowledge had come to him many years before, as he mentioned (see Alma 10:5). Let's review a few things that can help us continue to believe what we know, because continually choosing to believe will bring greater knowledge as our light and truth continue to grow (see Doctrine and Covenants 50:24).

Faithfully Framing Your Questions

Before launching into this section, it's important to point out that there are many incredible resources available for approaching concerns or new and potentially unsettling information about the Church or the gospel from a position of faith. In fact, the Church now has an official web page dedicated to "Church and Gospel Questions," where there are five guiding principles laid out for "Seeking Answers to Questions" and another five principles for "Helping Others with Questions."[4] One of the guiding principles for seeking answers to questions is to consult reliable sources, where clear instruction is given about evaluating the reliability of a source, learning to recognize bias, corroborating what you learn, and distinguishing facts from interpretation. When it comes to gospel questions, there are many powerful and practical perspectives worthy of reading.* My intent will not be to replicate or even summarize those great resources here, but to offer a brief perspective on the concept of faithfully framing questions.

We've now used the "experiment" from Alma's sermon to the Zoramites several times to explain how we receive our personal witness

---

* A few of the resources I highly recommend related to seeking answers to gospel questions are: (1) Lawrence E. Corbridge, "Stand Forever," BYU devotional, 22 January 2019; (2) David A. Bednar, "But We Heeded Them Not," *Liahona*, May 2022; (3) David A. Bednar, *Increase In Learning—Spiritual Patterns for Obtaining Your Own Answers* (Salt Lake City: Deseret Book, 2011); (4) Dieter F. Uchtdorf, "Come, Join with Us," *Ensign*, November 2013; (5) John Bytheway, *How Do I Know If I Know?* (Salt Lake City: Deseret Book, 2014); (6) Dieter F. Uchtdorf, "What Is Truth?" CES devotional address, 13 January 2013.

of gospel truth. Let's use the same sermon to identify how we can faithfully frame questions about information that we don't understand that may challenge our belief in what we know.

As a brief reminder, the invitation Alma makes is to "awake and arouse your faculties"—be alert and observant, prepared to make note of the impact of what you're about to do—and "exercise a particle of faith" (Alma 32:27) by planting the word, represented by a seed, in your heart (32:28). After planting this seed (the word of God) in a manner that demonstrates your faith, you will *observe* that it begins to grow. At this point, you *reason* that it must be a good seed, because it's growing, and this must then increase your faith that it's a good seed (see 32:30).

Now comes the first type of question. You've had this experience, you've noticed the seed is growing, and your belief in its truthfulness is increasing, but are you *sure*? "And now, behold, are ye sure that this is a good seed?" (Alma 32:31). The framing of this question comes from a position of doubt. Instead of standing firm in the belief of what you have observed, you begin questioning the reality of it all. *Is this just an emotional response? Am I simply being influenced by others?* These doubts are part of the pressures of the world weighing down on you, which Jesus identified as thorns in His parable of the sower, when He taught that they are "the cares of this world, and the deceitfulness of riches, and the lusts of other things entering in, chok[ing] the word, and it becometh unfruitful" (Mark 4:19).

Alma's answer here brings us back to the basics of what actually happened. Strip away all the distracting variables and just consider the result before you, which is that you planted the seed, it swelled and sprouted and began to grow, so "ye must needs *know* that the seed is good" (Alma 32:33; emphasis added). This is another reminder that the seed does not need to grow into a full fruit-bearing tree before we know it's good or true (see 32:28). The evidence from when it "beginneth to grow" is enough (32:33).

With this evidence, we now know the seed is good (i.e., the word is true), and our faith has become dormant or our knowledge "perfect in that thing" (Alma 32:34)—we all know what we personally experience. This is acknowledging the official transition from "not knowing" to "knowing," and if you know something, then believing it is no longer relevant. Importantly though, it is only perfect knowledge in *that thing* that has been planted—you don't know all things and thus must continue to have faith (see Alma 32:35–36).

What's more, as we explored above, *you must also continue to believe that you know*, otherwise you may fall into a situation of neglecting the tree that's now growing. If you "take no thought for [the tree's] nourishment, behold it will not get any root; and when the heat of the sun cometh and scorcheth it, because it hath no root it withers away, and ye pluck it up and cast it out" (Alma 32:38). The heat of the sun can be any of the circumstances or pressures we face in life that cause us to challenge what we know. It represents influences separate from us—external triggers—that without our ongoing faithfulness on the covenant path will damage the tree. However, it's crucial to recognize that these *external* influences didn't remove the tree from within us. No matter what is happening *to* us, we're still the only ones in charge of how we choose to *act*, which in the case of verse 38 involved us taking the tree that had sprouted from the word in our hearts and "pluck[ing] it up and cast[ing] it out" (32:38).

Let's rewind back to Alma 32:34, when we realize we know the seed is good because it has begun to enlighten us. I love the clarity of this as it relates to acting versus being acted upon. I've often mistakenly thought a witness from the Spirit confirming truth came exclusively from something tangible in the way that a growing seed is tangible. This could be a distinct feeling, a voice to our mind, or some other sign. However, what it says here is that it's the enlightening of our understanding and expansion of our mind that can also serve as the confirming witness. It's not something that acted upon us, but rather how we have now been *enabled to act*. Our view of life, the world, and our place in it has been elevated. Just as with the people of King Benjamin, "we have no more disposition to do evil, but to do good continually" (Mosiah 5:2) and we "have great views of that which is to come" (5:3). In other words, a change in our outlook on the world is a sign of the seed's growth, enlightening our mind, enabling us to act, and evidence the seed is good and that we "know of [its] surety and truth" (5:2).

Upon this recognition, the question of belief in what we know is revisited by Alma, but this time from a place of faith. Rather than asking with doubt if we are "sure" (Alma 32:31), we now ask, "O then, is not this real?" (32:35). The sun is still scorching, and the pressure of the naysayers remains, but our response is not to retreat to doubt. Instead, we pose the question from a place of *belief in what we know*—this is a faithfully framed question. It would be surprising to us for this *not* to be real after what we have observed and come to know—hence the question "is *not* this real?" (32:35, emphasis added).* This demonstrates the importance of not allowing our awareness of what we don't know to overshadow the truths we *do* know. Does the realization that you don't understand advanced calculus negate your knowledge of basic arithmetic? Does the awareness that you can't orchestrate a symphony diminish your ability to appreciate a philharmonic concert? Of course not.

In Helaman 5, when the brothers Nephi and Lehi were imprisoned by the Lamanites, there were magnificent manifestations from heaven seen by three hundred people. Pillars of fire surrounded each person without burning them, the "Holy Spirit of God" filled their hearts "as if with fire" (Helaman 5:45), they heard the voice of the Father declaring peace to them, and angels came down from heaven and ministered to

---

* This relates to our discussion in Chapter 8 about the phrasing of Moroni's promise in Moroni 10:4, where we are invited to ask "if these things are not true" based on the already present belief (or expectation) we have that they *are* true.

them. After all these visual, spiritual, and seemingly undeniable experiences, what instruction do they receive? They "were bidden to go forth and marvel not, *neither should they doubt*" (5:49; emphasis added). How could they possibly doubt after the magnificent outpouring they had just experienced? The answer is found in the ongoing importance of believing that which we come to know. No matter how we've come to the knowledge, the world will pressure us to doubt.

So What If Something Confusing or Troubling Challenges What You Know?

A reality of our time is that you *will* be confronted with information that challenges the things you've come to know as true. Faithfully framing your questions is an important first strategy and response to such information, but what do you do if your faithfully framed questions seem to go unanswered? Unfortunately, the next step is not easy (as with other things we've discussed, it is *simple* but *not easy*)—you should "wait on the Lord" (Psalm 27:14) without allowing the new information to rewrite your history. You made findings before as you planted a seed, exercised faith, observed growth, and gained knowledge along with a new outlook. The new information may add perspective or context to what you know, but these should be held separate from the core truth that God has spoken to you, for He cannot lie (see Enos 1:6).

I honestly wish I had a succinct and clear answer to why God's communications to us are often less noticeable than we may hope for, or why they may be lacking in comprehensive explanations. But what I do know is that if you believe the scriptures, it's clear that this is how He has always dealt with His children in mortality. Even those with some of the most clear and direct channels between earth and heaven, such as the Prophet Joseph Smith, have found themselves in situations of confusion about God's dealings or His divine silence. We may relate at times to Joseph as he pleaded from the confines of Liberty Jail, "O God, where art thou? And where is the pavilion that covereth thy hiding place?" (Doctrine and Covenants 121:1).

My overarching hope is that you will not let snapshots of shocking information pull you away from the covenant path and your belief in what you know.* As counseled on the Church's web page for "Seeking Answers to Questions," it is crucial to keep your life centered on Jesus Christ as you're patient with yourself (and others), recognizing that revelation is a process.[5] If you're troubled by something you've heard, dig deeper into factual and well-researched (i.e., reliable) resources;† if the concern relates to Church history, there are many excellent resources the Church has increasingly published in recent years.‡ Don't let something you don't understand, or even something you dislike, compromise your belief in what you know to be true. I recognize this is easier said than done—it's one of the most challenging battles of our day—but the reward for perseverance on the covenant path is worth the effort. Remember, in the armor of God our shield is *faith* (see Doctrine and Covenants 27:17 or Ephesians 6:16), as that's what is required if we

---

* Scott Woodward uses the following analogy to describe the danger of drawing conclusions from facts without understanding their full context: facts without context are like an electrical wire stripped of its insulation—when you come into contact with them, it can be shocking. I love this imagery (and not just because I'm an electrical engineer). He shares more about this in his podcast with Casey Griffiths called *Church History Matters*, available at https://doctrineandcovenantscentral.org/church-history-matters-podcast/; accessed 4 November 2024.

† Two of the many options to consider would be: (1) The Interpreter Foundation (www.interpreterfoundation.org), which supports, but is not affiliated with, the Church "through scholarship," and (2) the BYU Religious Studies Center (www.rsc.byu.edu), which has articles, books, and other resources available through their website. Both organizations have information accessible and searchable by topic and even by *Come, Follow Me* curriculum.

‡ Many resources exist, including all four volumes of *Saints: The Story of the Church of Jesus Christ in the Latter Days* and the extensive work of The Joseph Smith Papers (twenty-seven-volume set, plus more original documents and scholarship at josephsmithpapers.org).

are to protect ourselves from the high-pressure "fiery darts" that attack what we believe.

Don't Discount the Witnesses!

When you find yourself troubled and are asking faithfully framed questions, I encourage you to reflect on the witnesses the Lord has placed in your path. These could be family members, leaders, or friends who have been a light to you, demonstrating the fruits of a faithfully nourished tree in their hearts. Witnesses are sacred in God's plan, and He always provides them to support the essential truths of the gospel. Both the origin and sustenance of our knowledge of truth involves witnesses. As Paul taught, "how shall they believe in him of whom they have not heard? and how shall they hear without a preacher?" (Romans 10:14).

During my early days as a researcher, when I struggled to replicate the growth of the carbon nanotubes, I would occasionally turn to my mentor, who was also present on that remarkable day when the growth was successful. It served as a sort of sanity check for a truth in which I felt my belief waning. His confirming perspective always provided a much-needed boost of reassurance.

My wife, Lianne, had a powerful experience related to the three witnesses of the Book of Mormon who were visited by the angel Moroni and shown the gold plates. These witnesses were reputable men of their day, and they lived for decades never denying the glorious vision and corresponding truthfulness of the Book of Mormon. Lianne was the Gospel Doctrine teacher and while preparing her lessons, she developed the strongest desire to have just a few moments with one of the three witnesses to ask them directly if what they saw was real. This longing was constant, and she even lamented to me several times how much she wished she could go back in time to talk to one of them just for a few minutes. This went on for weeks when, during her gospel study, she unexpectedly stumbled across the story of William E. McLellin. In 1833, McLellin was with Oliver Cowdery and David Whitmer—two of the Three Witnesses—when they found themselves in a precarious situation where they feared for their lives during a period of intense persecution of Church members in Missouri. As they made a covert escape through the woods, McLellin took the opportunity to ask Cowdery and Whitmer about their testimonies of the Book of Mormon:

> I said to them, "brethren I never have seen an open vision in my life, but you men say you have, and therefore you positively know. Now you know that our lives are in danger every hour, if the mob can only catch us. Tell me in the fear of God, . . . is that book of Mormon true?" Cowdery looked at me with solemnity depicted in his face, and said, "Brother William, God sent his holy angel to declare the truth of the translation of it to us, and therefore we know. And though the mob kill us, yet we must die declaring its truth."*

For Lianne, being led to this little-known exchange was a tender mercy from the Lord. She felt an immediate kinship to William McLellin and knew this was an answer to her longing for another witness to what she already felt she knew. It provided her virtually the exact interaction she wished she could have.

Focus on Who We Have Come to Know

In all this discussion about what we know, whether we believe what we know, framing questions, and relying on witnesses, I wouldn't want

---

* Mitchell K. Schaefer, "'The Testimony of Men': William E. McLellin and the Book of Mormon Witnesses," *BYU Studies Quarterly*, vol. 50, no. 1 (2011): 109; available at https://scholarsarchive.byu.edu/byusq/vol50/iss1/9/; accessed 4 November 2024. It's also worth noting that a somewhat similar exchange occurred between Thomas B. Marsh and two of the Three Witnesses as recorded in his autobiography *History of Thomas Baldwin Marsh*, quoted in the excerpt available at https://whitmercollege.com /interviews/thomas-marsh-1838/; accessed 4 November 2024.

the most important aspect of coming to know gospel truth to be over-shadowed. You can tear out the four-quadrants diagram and cross out all the previous text in this chapter if it distracts you from this central aim: coming to know Jesus Christ, His grace, perfect love, and invitation to follow Him. After all, He is the seed planted in your heart in Alma's experiment, as Elder David A. Bednar explains:

> The seed we should strive to plant in our hearts is the word—even the life, mission, and doctrine of Jesus Christ. And as the word is nourished by faith, it can become a tree springing up *in us* unto everlasting life.
>
> What was the symbolism of the tree in Lehi's vision? The tree can be considered as a representation of Jesus Christ.
>
> My beloved brothers and sisters, is the Word in us? Are the truths of the Savior's gospel written in the fleshy tables of our hearts? Are we coming unto and gradually becoming more like Him? Is the tree of Christ growing in us? Are we striving to become "new [creatures]" in Him?[6]

I speak to myself as much as to anyone when I say: Let's do less diagramming and tallying of what we know and don't know. Instead, let's focus more on whom we have come to know through our spiritual experiments and defining moments. After all, He is "the way, the truth, and the life" (John 14:6). Coming to know Him as the capital *T* Truth is to embrace the most important, saving aspects of the gospel.† It means knowing that He is all merciful and that He came to make salvation possible. This is not a knowledge that includes understanding all the *hows*

---

† I called attention to this earlier, but I once again want to point to the 2019 Jeffrey L. Thayne and Edwin E. Gantt book, *Who Is Truth?* They provide a wonderfully thorough description of how Jesus Christ is the Truth we should be coming to know as a person, not some fixed, immovable piece of information but a living, loving, acting Truth that we can love and follow.

and *whens*—it is entirely about *who*. The only "who" that matters: for Him, that's you, and for all of us, it's Him.

Applying the Principles

1. **Revisit foundational truths:** Just as my initial successful growth of carbon nanotubes in the lab provided an undeniable proof of concept, we should revisit the foundational spiritual truths we've received. These early confirmations serve as anchors during times when new spiritual experiences may seem elusive. Regularly reflect on these moments to reinforce your faith and understanding.

2. **Believe what you know:** If you're struggling with something you've recently become aware of, faithfully frame your questions from a position of belief in what you already know. This will allow you to dig deeper into trusted and reputable resources for further understanding about this new information, until you find answers that are satisfactory or you move on with faith in what you have and trust that God will explain the rest in His time.

3. **Remember the witnesses:** You've likely had more than you realize. I encourage you to take a few moments to make a list of all the people who have been witnesses to you of the blessings of walking the covenant path (go ahead, write it right here in the margins). Whether or not these people are currently choosing to believe what they know or not, they have provided for you a witness of the reality of the good seed.

4. **Science cares most about process, but the gospel cares most about result:** The details of a scientific experiment are paramount. While the results may determine the level of interest in the experiment, the *process* is the most important component. In the gospel, however, the emphasis is different. While the process may involve a few key ingredients, it is deeply personalized, and what ultimately

matters most is the *result*—what we're becoming as a result of that process and a knowledge of the Son of God and the truths that flow from that knowledge. Be sure to stay focused on this result and not get too caught up in the process when it comes to gospel truths (though there can be important, life-changing things learned through the process itself).

5. **The seed is Christ, and the tree bears the fruit of His love:** As you finish the rest of Alma 32, you're reminded that the seed that was planted in your heart grows up to be the tree of life, whose fruit (growing within you) is the very love of God. Whenever you feel unmoored or distraught by the information you're bombarded with, return your focus to this most essential, central, and all-important truth. It's a truth you know, whether you know you know it or not.

I've had my moments of doubt in the things I know. Part of what's helped me through these times has been drawing an analogy to my experience running scientific experiments to grow carbon nanotubes. It may seem like a trivial example, but for me, it unified these two worlds of truth-finding. Comparing my planting of the gospel seed and observing its growth to my study of carbon nanotube growth brought clarity to the frustrations and doubts that have arisen over the years. I've found that continuously choosing to believe in what I know while navigating the swarm of information and misinformation allows me to feel more steady and supported by the Spirit of truth. Most importantly, an unwavering focus on the central truth—our Savior Jesus Christ—is what I've found to be the surest source of strength amid life's storms.

Chapter 10

FINDING PEACE IN THE TEMPEST

Whether the wrath of the storm-tossed sea
Or demons or men or whatever it be,
No waters can swallow the ship where lies
The Master of ocean and earth and skies.

—Mary Ann Baker

In the fall of 2012, Hurricane Sandy hammered the northeastern United States with eighty-mile-per-hour winds and storm surges that flooded many areas, including New York City. My family lived in the Lower Hudson Valley at the time, just forty miles north of the city, and during this hurricane a massive tree fell on our house, destroying our deck, damaging our roof, imploding a set of sliding-glass doors, and landing right in our kitchen—the sound was deafening. I'd just gone upstairs from the relative safety of our basement to get some water for our young children when the tree came down. I only narrowly escaped what would have no doubt been a life-changing or life-ending injury if I hadn't made a critical last-second decision to turn right instead of left when I entered the kitchen. For the rest of that night, we hunkered down in our basement to the sound of not just the hurricane outside our house, but inside it as well.

While this was quite traumatic for us, it didn't take long to realize that our damage was actually far less severe than many others in the area. In the weeks that followed, our congregation participated in cleanup efforts in the Rockaways in the borough of Queens, which was one of the areas devastated by flooding and fires throughout the night the storm hit. Hurricane Sandy is considered one of the top ten worst storms ever to hit the greater New York City area and remains one of the costliest storms in US history.[1] Having experienced a glimpse of how destructive a major storm can be, I've reflected over the years on the power and unpredictability of storms of all types.

What makes something a storm? It's not simply the presence of rain, snow, or wind. After all, a little rain is often welcome. A light breeze is usually pleasant. And an occasional moderate snowfall is just fine. But any of these elements in excess can wreak havoc.

Throughout this book, I've used the metaphor of a tumultuous storm to describe the overwhelming flood of information we face today. You don't need to go back to the dark ages to find a comparison that highlights the uniqueness of our current era. Consider the following differences just in the last twenty-five years, from 2000 to 2025:

- **Family, friends, and acquaintances.** In 2000, if you wanted to know how someone was doing, you had to call them, visit them in person, or happen to run into them while out and about. If the person was just an acquaintance, years might pass between updates. Now, in 2025, social media provides near-constant and far more detailed access to what's happening in the lives of everyone—from close family members to the person you haven't spoken to since the third grade. In just a thirty-second scroll, you can see updates from a sibling, a coworker, someone who didn't like you in middle school, a celebrity, and the person you met last week.
- **Media.** Twenty-five years ago, having a favorite series to watch meant recording the episodes when they aired once a week. Seeing a movie meant either renting or buying a DVD

or buying a ticket to the theater. Now, full seasons of series are released immediately, creating the era of binge-watching. Movies often drop straight to streaming services, and you have access to so many that the options are often more dizzying than exciting.

- **Political commentary and news in general.** A news junkie in the year 2000 was someone hooked on watching a cable news channel and/or who subscribed to several newspapers, either online or in physical form. Now, anyone with a social media app can join the fray of commentary about politics, world events, or just about anything else. What's more, our perceptions of people are unavoidably influenced by what we see them share or post, adding a level of complexity to our relationships that's often unhealthy or unhelpful. We often find ourselves thinking of people based on what they post rather than who they are.
- **Scientific research findings.** For my area of research alone— semiconductor devices—the number of scientific journals publishing research articles has increased by over twenty times in the last twenty-five years. Just imagine, twenty times more articles to have to consider when seeking to understand what's been studied on a specific topic.

Elder Lawrence E. Corbridge summed up the storm of information raging upon us in our day as follows:

> Never has there been more information, misinformation, and disinformation; more goods, gadgets, and games; and more options, places to go, and things to see and do to occupy time and attention away from what is most important. And all of that and much more is disseminated instantaneously throughout the world by electronic media. This is a day of deception.[2]

As if this horrendous downpour of information weren't difficult enough, we have experiences and circumstances in life that bring storms of pain and sorrow upon us, spiritually and emotionally. Sickness or the loss of a loved one, seemingly insurmountable financial distress, or the disintegration of a cherished relationship can be like raging tornadoes to our previously clear skies of focused faith and truth, tossing them every which way.

In the midst of this war of words and tumult of confusion, what are we to do? Principles have been suggested throughout this book for how to approach the noise and uncertainty that may arise. After considering all of these, which I hope may be helpful for some, there are two principles that stand out most vividly to me: choosing to believe and focusing on Christ.

What we choose to believe amid the temporal sphere of information defines how we see the world and, in some respects, how we're viewed by others. Without the ability to reliably verify much of what we see or hear, we're often left with a simple choice: to believe it or not. The choice to believe gives great power to the information and the informant, but it does not determine whether the thing is truly accurate. Many pundits have gained fame and visibility by climbing a mountain of misinformation marketed as truth. Often, the mere alignment of information with our existing beliefs (i.e., biases) is enough for us to accept it as true. While I've offered a few principles that may help with navigating this dangerous aspect of our world today, I don't claim to have provided a definitive cure or philosophy. If there's one thing that's most important, it's that we do not allow what someone else believes to alter our view and treatment of them as a son or daughter of God. Let the two great commandments (see Matthew 22:37–40) be the guiding principles by which we navigate, maintaining access to our place of peace with Christ.

What is of far greater import than what we choose to believe about information in the temporal world is what we believe about and act on of the most essential truths, those of the gospel of Jesus Christ. These final sections will center the focus on the Savior, the power of believing in Him, and the reality of His watchful protection and care for us as we endure the storms of life. As Elder Neil L. Andersen taught:

> We are on the quest to live eternally with God. In our very secular and increasingly wicked world, we keep our feet firmly planted in our faith in Jesus Christ and in our desire to be with Him eternally, not allowing the distractions of our mortal life to overcome our efforts to become more and more like Jesus.[3]

Believing Brings Great Power

Earlier in the book, I mentioned how astonished I have recently been by the role and power of believing throughout the scriptures. Some may wonder why something so obvious would be surprising, since belief and faith (that is, taking action on belief) are central to almost any theology. However, with so much emphasis on *knowing* things, as often expressed in the language of Latter-day Saint testimonies, I have become more attuned to the significant role that *believing* plays.

In some instances, choosing to believe may stem from not having received a confirming witness, thereby necessitating the decision to either believe or not. Even when we've received a confirming witness from planting the word of God in our hearts, there are still times when we must choose to believe in what we know. Many of these moments arise when the storms of life surge upon us, bringing a downpour of unanticipated misinformation, suffering, or other distractions. One of the casualties of such storms may be our own confidence in the core gospel truths we'd previously come to know.

My point is: It's more than "just okay" to believe, it's powerful! Unless there's some deeper interpretation of what appears to be consistent and direct scriptural language, I suggest that the scriptures support this doctrine. *Knowing* that the word of God is true is stabilizing and power-ful, and *believing* that the word of God is true is ennobling and equally powerful. The same blessing of "eternal life if they continue faithful" (Doctrine and Covenants 46:14) is available to those who believe that Jesus Christ is their Savior as it is to those who are "given by the Holy Ghost to know" this same truth (see 46:11–14). A summary of notable instances in the scriptures where someone is asked about their belief, responds with a profession of belief, and then receives a blessing is pro-vided in Table 1.

Table 1. Examples from scripture of when someone is asked about their belief, they re-spond with a profession of belief, and then receive a resultant blessing. These demonstrate how choosing to believe and professing that belief carries great, ennobling power.

Reference	Asking	Responding	Result
1 Nephi 11:4–6	Spirit of the Lord: "Believest thou that thy father saw the tree of which he hath spoken?"	Nephi: "Yea, thou knowest that I believe all the words of my father."	Nephi is shown the vision of the tree, sees the Savior, and many glorious things.
Alma 45:2–8	Alma the Younger: "Believest thou in Jesus Christ, who shall come?"	Helaman (son of Alma): "Yea, I believe all the words which thou hast spo-ken."	Alma blesses Helaman and entrusts him with the sacred records.
Mosiah 4:9–5:9	King Benjamin: "Believe in God; believe that he is, and that he created all things"	Nephites: "We believe all the words which thou has spoken unto us; and also, we know of their surety and truth"	The people have no more disposition to do evil, great views of that which is to come, and they become the children of Christ (spiritu-ally begotten).
Matthew 9:28–29	Jesus: "Believe ye that I am able to do this?"	Two blind men: "Yea, Lord."	Jesus heals their blindness.

Mark 9:23–24	Jesus: "If thou canst believe, all things are possible to him that believeth."	Father of the possessed child: "Lord, I believe; help thou mine unbelief."	Jesus casts out the unclean spirit from the child.
John 11:26–27	Jesus: "Whosoever . . . believeth in me shall never die. Believest thou this?"	Martha: "Yea, Lord: I believe that thou art the Christ, the Son of God."	Jesus raises Martha's brother, Lazarus, from the dead.

In addition to these specific interactions with expressions of belief bringing about blessings, there are many other promises to those who believe. These include:

- "All things are possible to him that believeth" (Mark 9:23).
- "Whosoever believeth in [Christ] should . . . have everlasting life" (John 3:16).
- "Whosoever believeth in [Christ] shall receive remission of sins" (Acts 10:43).
- "Abraham believed God, and it was counted unto him for righteousness" (Romans 4:3).
- "Whoso believeth in God might with surety hope for a better world, yea, even a place at the right hand of God" (Ether 12:4).

Choosing to believe in the word of God, which is in Christ, opens the way for the blessings of heaven in our lives. As Elder L. Whitney Clayton testified of so powerfully:

Every day each of us faces a test. It is the test of our lifetimes: will we choose to believe in Him and allow the light of His gospel to grow within us[?] . . . The decision to believe [in Jesus Christ] is the most important choice we ever make. It shapes all our other decisions. . . . We will not accidentally come to believe in the Savior and His gospel any more than we will accidentally pray or pay tithing. We actively choose to believe, just like we choose to keep other commandments.[4]

Choosing to believe in Christ is an action most succinctly called *faith.* Making this choice links us to heaven—it's the act of holding fast to the word of God, which is Christ—and leads us to greater truth. What's more, this linkage keeps us on the Rock or Foundation that will protect us "when the devil shall send forth his mighty winds, yea, his shafts in the whirlwind, yea, when all his hail and his mighty storm shall beat upon [us]" so that all this "will have no power over [us] to drag [us] down to the gulf of misery and endless wo, because of the rock upon which [we] are built, which is a sure foundation, a foundation whereon if men build they cannot fall" (Helaman 5:12).

Finding Peace in the Tempest

Due to its geographical setting, the Sea of Galilee is known for sudden and violent storms. It sits in a basin surrounded by hills, which can cause sudden windstorms when cool air from the surrounding mountains rushes down to the warm air over the lake. These storms can be intense and frightening, as "in a matter of minutes, [the] gusts of wind transform the smooth surface of the water into a seething and roaring cauldron . . . the hurricane collides with the mountains that close off the eastern shore and merges with the winds that continue blowing, such that a hurricane can form in an instant."[5]

It appears just such a storm struck the Sea of Galilee as Jesus and His disciples were crossing one night. An unexpected tempest began to rage, burying the ship—likely a modest fishing vessel, given many of the disciples' former profession—and causing fear and panic among them. All the while, Jesus slept in the "hinder part" (Mark 4:38), or lower region of the ship. The fact that He was able to sleep amid such tumult seems indicative of many things, not the least of which is how very exhausted He must have been. Fearing for their lives, the disciples woke Jesus and asked, "Master, carest thou not that we perish?" (4:38). Jesus then "said unto the sea, Peace, be still" and "there was a great calm" (4:39).

This entire traumatic event is described in a mere five verses in Matthew and seven verses in Mark, yet they offer great insight into the circumstances of one of Jesus's most remarkable miracles. I find the correlation to how we react to the unexpected storms of life to be quite compelling. Let's walk through the account in Matthew 8:

> And when he was entered into a ship, *his disciples followed him.* (Matthew 8:23; emphasis added)

The disciples all started in the right place—they were following the Savior. This is a reminder that walking the covenant path to become like Jesus does not mean our lives will be free of storms and tempests.

> And, behold, there arose *a great tempest in the sea,* insomuch that the ship was covered with the waves: *but he was asleep.* (Matthew 8:24; emphasis added)

Then the storm hit. Just like being smacked with waves of information and misinformation, shouts of "Lo, here!" and "Lo, there!" or miseries and sorrows from the unexpected ailments of life. It wasn't just **water annoyingly splashing at or soaking them**—their entire ship was engulfed in waves, much like how it can feel when we're consumed by the torrent of noise and distraction the world tosses at us, seeking to rip us from the safety of our familiar ship and into the raging sea. I'm sure many of us have felt a level of confusion and/or sorrow that causes the very foundation on which we are standing to feel unstable.

And yet, amid the torrent, the Master slept. Let's bring the next verse in for contrast:

And his disciples came to him, and awoke him, saying, *Lord, save us: we perish.* (Matthew 8:25; emphasis added)

While the disciples feared they were about to lose everything, Jesus was able to sleep. This suggests that despite the raging storm, *there was always calm available on the ship.* In the same exact conditions through which Jesus was sleeping, the disciples were fearing for their lives—the *Rashomon* effect.

And he saith unto them, *Why are ye fearful, O ye of little faith?* Then he arose, and rebuked the winds and the sea; and *there was a great calm.* (Matthew 8:26; emphasis added)

Again, calm had been there and available to the disciples all along, but it was difficult for them to see it amid the waves. Once the waves of distraction were removed, the calm was then "great," or evident to all.

But the men marvelled, saying, What manner of man is this, that even the winds and the sea obey him! (Matthew 8:27)

Even though they had seen the Lord perform many miracles, the disciples were astonished by His ability to command the winds and the waves, saying, "Peace, be still" (Mark 4:39) and have them obey. Earlier that same day, as recorded in the book of Matthew, Jesus had healed a leper, a centurion's servant, and Peter's mother-in-law (see Matthew 8:1–15). That evening, "they brought unto him many that were possessed with devils: and he cast out the spirits with his word, and healed all that were sick" (Matthew 8:16). Despite witnessing all these miracles in one day, Jesus's disciples still did not fully grasp the extent of His power. The peace and understanding He brought were not just for the heart. He was not only the Master Teacher, Miraculous Healer, and Savior of their souls; He was and is the Master of the Universe, with authority over all things, thoughts, and events that occur within it.

I acknowledge that it can be difficult to realize how Jesus could have comprehension of, and power over, all the actions, comments, and claims that fill our world. *Yet He does.* It can seem unfathomable that He would have power to bring calm and peace when life feels ripped apart by sin, pain, or grief over unimaginable loss. *But He can.* He knows all that we can possibly come to know, and so much more that we cannot fathom. I choose to believe this.

> He that ascended up on high, as also he descended below all things, in that he comprehended all things, that he might be in all and through all things, the light of truth. (Doctrine and Covenants 88:6)

From Fear to Faith

The talented artist Howard Lyon painted my favorite depiction of this story of Jesus calming the tempest, titled "From Fear to Faith."[6] In the painting, Jesus is standing at the stern of the ship with a brilliant light visible behind Him, where the storm clouds are receding. As your eyes move away from Jesus, toward the other end of the ship, the painting darkens and a range of different behaviors are depicted among the disciples. Closest to the Master is Peter, who is kneeling and looking earnestly to the Lord. At the far end of the ship there is a disciple who is still bailing out water with a bucket, his back turned to Jesus. A few others still have one or both hands engaged in efforts to try and save the ship, but have their faces turned to look at the Savior. Per the title of the piece, the disciples from one end of the ship to the other display a transition from fear to faith, with focus on Christ. On the artist's website, the following description is provided for the painting:

> We will all face trials in this life. There will be times when the sea is raging around us. It may feel as if we are destined to fail, that the storms are too great and that we are helpless. This painting

depicts a range of emotions that we may all relate to when trials come.

We will all face difficult moments in our life, when it feels that all is lost. We often try to save ourselves, but when we turn ourselves over to the Lord, having done all that we can, He will save us.

We will hear those magnificent words spoken in our hearts, *"Peace, be still."*[7]

As I think back on the difficulties I've faced in life, I can see myself in each of the disciples depicted in Lyon's painting. Of one thing I'm certain: the times when I weathered the storm with my focus on Christ, choosing to believe in His peace, were far brighter and better, not necessarily due to miraculous deliverance but thanks to finding calm amid the storm. As Elder John Groberg so beautifully relates about an experience he had as a missionary serving in Tonga: "Sometimes God calms the storm and sometimes He calms His child."[8]

Master, the Tempest Is Raging

The lyrics for the hymn "Master, the Tempest Is Raging" were penned by Mary Ann Baker in 1874 at the request of the composer H. R. Palmer. He'd asked for songs that matched the Bible Sunday School theme for the year, "Christ Stilling the Tempest." Baker noted that the theme "so expressed an experience I had recently passed through, that this hymn was the result." She had endured incredible hardship in her life, including losing both of her parents to tuberculosis and then having her only brother stricken by the same disease. Baker and her sister gathered all the money they had and sent their brother from their home in Chicago down to Florida in hopes that it would improve his health. However, within a few weeks, he died, and they could not afford to visit him or bring his body back home. Baker related the following:

For two weeks the long lines of telegraph wires carried back and forth messages between the dying brother and his waiting sisters, ere the word came which told us that our beloved brother was no longer a dweller on the earth.

Although we mourned not as those without hope, and although I had believed on Christ in early childhood and had always desired to give the Master a consecrated and obedient life, I became wickedly rebellious at this dispensation of divine providence. I said in my heart that God did not care for me or mine. But the Master's own voice stilled the tempest in my unsanctified heart, and brought it to the calm of a deeper faith and a more perfect trust.[9]

With Baker's lyrics set to music by H. R. Palmer, the hymn quickly rose in popularity among Christian faiths, appearing in more than 250 hymnals.[10] The powerful words capture the deep struggle and emotion of the disciples as they endured the storm in verses 1 and 2, while the chorus reminds the listener of the Master's power and presence. The final verse describes the peace that follows the calming of the storm, with the plea, "Linger, O blessed Redeemer! / Leave me alone no more."[11]

While Hurricane Sandy brought unexpected chaos to my family's life in 2012, there have been less physical but far more intense storms that have raged in my life over the years. Some of these storms have engulfed my entire family in waves of concern or pain, while others have attacked me individually with disappointment, confusion, or doubt. Through these storms, I have witnessed undeniable miracles in my life and in the lives of my family members; these miracles are evidence to me that within our family's ship lies the Master, even Jesus Christ, who can bring peace to any panic and calm to any calamity.

Since Mary Ann Baker penned the words to "Master, the Tempest Is Raging," many arrangements and new musical accompaniments have been composed for the hymn. One of these has profoundly impacted my soul, written by my wife, Lianne. While the original music for the hymn has an upbeat tempo with a light and airy feel, her composition reflects the emotions of the verses, with a more somber tone in the first two verses, the acknowledgment and reassurance of the chorus, and the relief and joy of the final verse. Listening to Lianne's inspired composition brings clarity and a deep awareness of the Lord's presence in my life and His ability to bring calm to any of life's storms, whether they be a deluge of information, a torrent of doubt, or a whirlwind of pain.

Not being a musician myself, I lack the ability to fully describe just how beautifully Lianne's composition connects with Mary Ann Baker's lyrics in a way that so vividly speaks to the soul. I know it involves the use of minor keys, major keys, tempo, chords, and other musical elements, but the reality is the result is so much greater than the sum of its parts. There is no song that has brought more meaning and a more faithful perspective to my life. This was cemented in my soul when I heard the song performed at Temple Square in Salt Lake City.* This performance allowed you to truly feel the swells of wind and waves and experience the peace that comes from the Master. A recording is available on the Church's website.[12] I encourage you to take a moment to listen to it as you reflect on the storms that may be raging in your life and consider the Master who can bring peace and calm.

Applying the Principles

1. **No storm can swallow the ship where lies the Master:** Look to Him. Believe what you know *about* Him and *because* of Him. Do not allow any other forces to separate you from His love. All other pursuits of knowledge and understanding can be improved by keeping an uncompromised focus on Jesus and seeking to be more like Him.
2. **Embrace the power of believing:** Never feel ashamed to "only"

---

* The song was performed at the annual Church Music Festival by an institute choir led by Ryan Eggett in the Assembly Hall at Temple Square.

believe in the gospel of Jesus Christ. Choosing to believe brings tremendous power. Express the things you *know* to be true because you *believe* in what you have witnessed, and you believe what you know.

3. **Do not limit God:** On the tumultuous Sea of Galilee that fear-filled night, the disciples learned not to limit what the Master is capable of. We can learn profound lessons from their experience. There is no field of knowledge, current or past, of which He is not perfectly aware. Increase your trust in Him and prioritize holding onto His word, and you can also find calm on the seas. The storm itself may not be calmed, but your mind and heart can be.

It may seem like there's no end to the questions you face, the obstacles you encounter, or the confusion that this information-packed world causes. Yet regardless of how turbulent the storm, the answer is simple—not easy, but simple. As President Russell M. Nelson so perfectly taught:

> Whatever questions or problems you have, the answer is always found in the life and teachings of Jesus Christ. Learn more about His Atonement, His love, His mercy, His doctrine, and His restored gospel of healing and progression. Turn to Him! Follow Him![13]

Note that he does not indicate any caveat here. It's not "whatever questions, unless they are about physics" or "whatever problems, unless it's about relationships"—there's no limit. The life and teachings of Jesus Christ are the word of God to which we should be holding fast. As we do so, pressing forward on the covenant path to become more like Him, we will be led to greater truth and light. Our path will be straight, while generating a perfect round that circumscribes *all* truth into one great whole.

Want to know more about science? Look to Jesus, hold firm to His word, and seek for greater understanding without letting go. Want to cut through the clutter of political opinion and know what to do? Be uncompromising in following the Master, who ignored worldly labels when He lived on the earth and taught that our love for God and for others should be the guiding principle to every other thought we have or action we take. Want to turn fear to faith, pain to peace, and calamity to calm? Lay hold upon the word of God, which is Christ. Never forget that "no waters can swallow the ship where lies / The Master of ocean and earth and skies."[14]

ACKNOWLEDGMENTS

"I'm thinking about writing another book." This must be one of the most dreaded statements a person can hear from a friend or loved one who's an author. It took me weeks to muster the courage to say this to friends and family—people I knew I would rely on for feedback if I chose to embark on another writing journey. Little did they know, their reactions to this statement would play a significant role in my decision to move forward. I owe my sincere thanks to Lianne, Rich, and Jake for not responding, "Are you sure that's a good idea?"

Before the metaphorical pen touched paper, this book was born from countless meaningful and thought-provoking discussions with others. From very personal one-on-one conversations and Sunday School discussions to inspiring sacrament meeting talks and podcasts, the individuals whose thoughts have shaped my perspectives and ideas are far too many to name.

I am deeply grateful to those who took the time to read various versions of this manuscript, including Lianne Franklin, Jake Smith, Rich Jones, Claudia Walters, Steve Walters, and (Hermana) Ellie Franklin. Your time and critical feedback were invaluable—truly, you helped bring this book to life. It was especially fun to receive comments from my daughter while she was serving as a full-time missionary!

The team at Deseret Book has been absolutely fantastic to work with. My genuine thanks to Lisa Roper for her initial strong encouragement and to Janiece Johnson for her patience and helpful feedback as the manuscript moved from a one-page synopsis to a full-length book. I am also grateful to Derk Koldewyn for superb editing and the rest of the Deseret Book team who contributed to bringing the diagrams (some of them rather silly) to a quality final product.

When I finally sat down to write this book, pulling together pages of scattered notes, I was visiting my mom shortly after she started hospice care. I would be sitting at her kitchen table, looking out at the beautiful Arizona desert behind her house, and from her bed across the room she would occasionally ask me how it was going. I'd read her a paragraph or share a story I had recently written into the book, and she would always respond, "Wow, that is so good, sweetie. I love it." Nothing I have ever done—or will ever do—can escape the loving support of my mom. I am forever grateful for her simple, pure, and ever-predictable approval. Believing came naturally to Mom, and her exemplary faith has had an incredible impact on me that I hope comes through in the book.

It is no coincidence that my wife, Lianne, features prominently in more than half the chapters of this book. It's not because she inserted herself—quite the opposite, she encouraged me to leave her out! Her presence in these pages reflects the countless discussions we've had over the years about truth and how to find it. Her insights have profoundly shaped my views and understanding. But her contributions go beyond her wisdom. Lianne offered unwavering encouragement and support during the moments I doubted whether this book should be written. No one understands better what a struggle this was, and no one served as a greater beacon of guidance than she did. To me, the most significant and powerful messages in this book owe their origin to her. Lianne, thank you for your patience, selflessness, and invaluable feedback. I love you.

NOTES

Chapter 1

Epigraph: T. S. Eliot, "Choruses from 'The Rock'"; in *The Complete Poems and Plays: 1909–1950* (New York: Harcourt, Brace & World, 1934), 96.

1. *Lectures on Faith* (1985).
2. David A. Bednar, "But We Heeded Them Not," *Liahona*, May 2022.
3. *Lectures on Faith*, 3:2.

Chapter 2

Epigraph: Quoted in Gabriel Meyer, "Pontifical Science Academy Banks on Stellar Cast," *National Catholic Register*, December 1–7 (North Haven, CT: Circle Media, Inc., 1996). Dr. Murray was a founder of organ transplantation and performed the first kidney transplant.

1. Russell M. Nelson, "The Tie Between Science and Religion," address given at dedication of the Brigham Young University Life Sciences Building, 9 April 2015; available at https://speeches.byu.edu/talks/russell-m-nelson/the-tie-between-science-and -religion/; accessed 6 January 2025.

Chapter 3

Epigraph: Russell M. Nelson, "Pure Truth, Pure Doctrine, and Pure Revelation," *Liahona*, November 2021.

1. Spencer W. Kimball, "Absolute Truth," BYU devotional, 6 September 1977; available at https://speeches.byu.edu/talks/spencer-w-kimball/absolute-truth/; accessed 6 January 2025.
2. D. Todd Christofferson, "Truth Endures," address to CES religious educators, 26 January 2018; available at https://rsc.byu.edu/vol-19-no-3-2018/truth-endures; accessed 6 January 2025.
3. Joseph E. Murray, *Surgery of the Soul: Reflections on a Curious Career* (New York: Science History Publications/USA, 2004).
4. Scott R. Frazer, *Where Science Meets God: 12 Ways Science Reinforces LDS Doctrine* (Springville, UT: Cedar Fort, 2018).

5. Spencer W. Kimball, "Absolute Truth."

6. **Dieter F. Uchtdorf, "Nourish the Roots, and the Branches Will Grow,"** *Liahona,* **November 2024.**

7. John C. Pingree Jr., "Eternal Truth," *Liahona,* November 2023.

8. See https://www.churchofjesuschrist.org/study/manual/gospel-topics/seeking -answers/02-center-your-life-on-jesus-christ?lang=eng; accessed 9 October 2024.

Chapter 4

Epigraph: Mark D. Eddy, "The Virtue of the Word," *Liahona,* November 2022.

1. Quoted in Charlotte Larcabal, "President and Sister Nelson's Devotional for Youth: Keep on the Covenant Path," *New Era,* March 2019.

2. D. Todd Christofferson, "Why the Covenant Path," *Liahona,* May 2021.

3. Joy D. Jones, "An Especially Noble Calling," *Ensign,* May 2020; see embedded video and transcript.

4. Michelle D. Craig, "Wholehearted," *Liahona,* November 2022.

5. Mark D. Eddy, "The Virtue of the Word."

Chapter 5

Epigraph: Gary B. Sabin, "Hallmarks of Happiness," *Liahona,* November 2023.

1. Russell M. Nelson, "Peacemakers Needed," *Liahona,* May 2023.

2. Gary E. Stevenson, "Bridging the Two Great Commandments," *Liahona,* May 2024.

3. Dieter F. Uchtdorf, "What Is Truth?" CES devotional address, 13 January 2013; available at https://speeches.byu.edu/talks/dieter-f-uchtdorf/what-is-truth/.

Chapter 6

Epigraph: James R. Hansen, *First Man: The Life of Neil A. Armstrong* (New York: Simon & Schuster, 2005).

1. Myles Burke, "Apollo 11 launch: 'If you can survive the simulations, the mission is a piece of cake,'" *BBC,* 15 July 2024; available at https://www.bbc.com/culture/article /20240712-it-was-no-longer-training-it-was-real-the-same-emotions-the-same -feelings-the-same-adrenaline-would-flow; accessed 31 October 2024.

2. *Apollo 11 moon landing: Minute by minute,* Royal Museums Greenwich, n.d.; available at https://www.rmg.co.uk/stories/topics/apollo-11-moon-landing-minute-minute; accessed 28 July 2024.

3. Dieter F. Uchtdorf, "Jesus Christ Is the Strength of Youth," *Liahona,* November 2022.

4. Nir Eyal, "Learn How To Avoid Distraction In A World That Is Full Of It," *Nir and Far* (website); available at https://www.nirandfar.com/distractions/; accessed 4 March 2024.

5. Nir Eyal, "Learn How To Avoid Distraction In A World That Is Full Of It."

Chapter 7

Epigraph: Oscar Wilde, *Lady Windermere's Fan* (London: Methuen & Co., 1893).
1. Bruce R. McConkie, "The Lord's People Receive Revelation," *Ensign*, June 1971.
2. Russell M. Nelson, "Hear Him," *Ensign*, May 2020.
3. Quentin L. Cook, "Looking beyond the Mark," *Ensign*, March 2003.
4. Boyd K. Packer, "The Candle of the Lord," *Ensign*, January 1983.
5. Kyle S. McKay, "A Sure and Certain Foundation," BYU-Idaho devotional, 25 April 2023; available at https://www.byui.edu/speeches/kyle-s-mckay/a-sure-and-certain-foundation; accessed 4 November 2024.
6. Penelope Moody Allen, "Let the Holy Spirit Guide," *Hymns* (Salt Lake City: The Church of Jesus Christ of Latter-day Saints, 1985), no. 143. © by Intellectual Reserve, Inc.

Chapter 8

Epigraph: The origin of this famous quote is unknown. Though it is commonly attributed to Henry David Thoreau, it doesn't appear verbatim in any of his writings. Many think it captures his philosophy on perception and perspective. The closest official reference that aligns with the sentiment of the quote is from Thoreau's journal entry on August 5, 1851: "The question is not what you look at—but how you look and whether you see," as available in: Henry David Thoreau, *The Writings of Henry David Thoreau: Journal* (Boston and New York: Houghton Mifflin, 1906).
1. "History of the Royal Society," *RoyalSociety.org* (website); available at https://royalsociety.org/about-us/who-we-are/history/; accessed 5 February 2024.
2. See David McCullough, *The Wright Brothers* (New York: Simon & Schuster, 2015).
3. Dale G. Renlund, "Observation, Reason, Faith, and Revelation," BYU Education Week devotional, 22 August 2023; available at https://speeches.byu.edu/talks/dale-g-renlund/observation-reason-faith-and-revelation/; accessed 4 November 2024.
4. Russell M. Nelson, "What Is True?" *Liahona*, November 2022.
5. David A. Bednar, "If Ye Had Known Me," *Ensign*, November 2016.

Chapter 9

Epigraph: David A. Bednar, "If Ye Had Known Me," *Ensign*, November 2016.
1. David A. Bednar, "If Ye Had Known Me."
2. Quoted in J. S. Atherton, "Knowing and Not Knowing," *Doceo*, available at https://www.doceo.co.uk/tools/knowing.htm; accessed March 5, 2024.
3. Lisa K. Fazio, "Repetition Increases Perceived Truth Even for Known Falsehoods," Collabra: Psychology, 6:38, 2020.
4. See https://www.churchofjesuschrist.org/life/church-and-gospel-questions?lang=eng; accessed 4 November 2024; this is also covered in Ryan Jensen, "Guiding Principles to Help Answer Gospel Questions," *Church News*, 16 December 2023; available at https://

www.thechurchnews.com/living-faith/2023/12/16/24004224/guiding-principles
-to-help-answer-gospel-questions-topics/; accessed 4 November 2024.

5. See https://www.churchofjesuschrist.org/life/church-and-gospel-questions
?lang=eng; accessed 4 November 2024.

6. David A. Bednar, "Abide in Me, and I in You; Therefore, Walk with Me," *Liahona*,
May 2023.

Chapter 10

Epigraph: Mary Ann Baker, "Master, the Tempest Is Raging," *Hymns* (Salt Lake City:
The Church of Jesus Christ of Latter-day Saints, 1985), no. 105.

1. "New List of the Costliest US Hurricanes Includes 2017's Harvey, Irma, Maria," *The
Weather Channel* (website), 29 January 2018; available at https://weather.com/storms
/hurricane/news/2018–01–29-americas-costliest-hurricanes; accessed 4 November
2024.

2. Lawrence E. Corbridge, "Stand Forever," BYU devotional, 22 January 2019; available
at https://speeches.byu.edu/talks/lawrence-e-corbridge/stand-for-ever/; accessed
4 November 2024.

3. Neil L. Andersen, "Educating Our Righteous Desires," BYU Education Week devotional, 20 August, 2024; available at https://speeches.byu.edu/talks/neil-l-andersen
/educating-our-righteous-desires/; accessed 4 November 2024.

4. L. Whitney Clayton, "Choose to Believe," Ensign, May 2015.

5. Alfonso Sánchez Lamadrid, "The Storms at the Sea of Galilee," *Saxum Visitor Center*
(website), 13 July 2023; available at https://www.saxum.org/the-storms-at-the-sea
-of-galilee/; accessed 4 November 2024.

6. See "From Fear to Faith," *HowardLyon.com* (website); available at https://www.howard
lyon.com/fineart-store/from-fear-to-faith; accessed 4 November 2024.

7. "From Fear to Faith," *HowardLyon.com*.

8. John H. Groberg, *The Other Side of Heaven* (Salt Lake City: Deseret Book, 2001).

9. Ira D. Sankey, *My Life and the Story of the Gospel Hymns and of Sacred Songs and
Solos* (New York: P. W. Ziegler, 1907), 220.

10. See "Mary Ann Baker," *Wikipedia.org* (website); available at https://en.wikipedia.org
/wiki/Mary_Ann_Baker; accessed 4 November 2024.

11. Mary Ann Baker, "Master, the Tempest Is Raging," *Hymns*, no. 105.

12. "Master, the Tempest Is Raging," Music Library, *ChurchofJesusChrist.org* (website);
available at https://www.churchofjesuschrist.org/media/music/songs/master-the
-tempest-is-raging-franklin?lang=eng; accessed 4 November 2024.

13. Russell M. Nelson, "The Answer Is Always Jesus Christ," *Liahona*, May 2023.

14. Mary Ann Baker, "Master, the Tempest Is Raging," *Hymns*, no. 105.